First World War
and Army of Occupation
War Diary
France, Belgium and Germany

41 DIVISION
122 Infantry Brigade
Hampshire Regiment
15th (Service) Battalion
1 March 1918 - 31 March 1919

WO95/2634/5

The Naval & Military Press Ltd
www.nmarchive.com
Published in association with The National Archives

Published by

The Naval & Military Press Ltd

Unit 10 Ridgewood Industrial Park,

Uckfield, East Sussex,

TN22 5QE England

Tel: +44 (0) 1825 749494

www.naval-military-press.com

www.nmarchive.com

This diary has been reprinted in facsimile from the original. Any imperfections are inevitably reproduced and the quality may fall short of modern type and cartographic standards.

© **Crown Copyright**
Images reproduced by permission of The National Archives, London, England, 2015.

Contents

Document type	Place/Title	Date From	Date To
Heading	WO95/2634/6		
Heading	15th Battn. The Hampshire Regiment. March1918		
War Diary	S. Martino	01/03/1918	03/03/1918
War Diary	France Warlingcourt	04/03/1918	08/03/1918
War Diary	Warlincourt	09/03/1918	21/03/1918
War Diary	Achiet-Le-Grand	22/03/1918	27/03/1918
War Diary	Bienvillers-au-Bois	28/03/1918	31/03/1918
Heading	15th Battalion The Hampshire Regiment April 1918		
Miscellaneous	Headquarters, 122nd Infantry Brigade	02/04/1918	02/04/1918
War Diary	Essars	01/04/1918	01/04/1918
War Diary	Marieux	02/04/1918	02/04/1918
War Diary	Orville	03/04/1918	03/04/1918
War Diary	Poperinghe	04/04/1918	04/04/1918
War Diary	School Camp	05/04/1918	07/04/1918
War Diary	Passchendaele Sector	08/04/1918	11/04/1918
War Diary	Passchendaele	12/04/1918	16/04/1918
War Diary	Ypres	17/04/1918	26/04/1918
War Diary	Orillia Camp.	27/04/1918	30/04/1918
Miscellaneous	Headquarters, 122nd Infantry Brigade.	03/06/1918	03/06/1918
War Diary		01/05/1918	31/05/1918
War Diary	Ypres	01/06/1918	03/06/1918
War Diary	Proven	04/06/1918	04/06/1918
War Diary	Ouestmount	05/06/1918	25/06/1918
War Diary	Watou	26/06/1918	28/06/1918
War Diary	Remy	29/06/1918	29/06/1918
War Diary	La Clytte	30/07/1918	30/07/1918
Miscellaneous	Appendix		
War Diary	La Clytte Sector.	01/07/1918	31/07/1918
Operation(al) Order(s)	Battalion Operation Order No. 122 by Lieut-Colonel C. Hurdoch D.S.O. Commanding "Branch"	22/07/1918	22/07/1918
Miscellaneous	Officer Commanding	03/09/1918	03/09/1918
War Diary	La Clytte	01/08/1918	31/08/1918
War Diary	Lumbres	01/09/1918	01/09/1918
War Diary	Abeele	02/09/1918	02/09/1918
War Diary	Vierstraat	03/09/1918	05/09/1918
War Diary	Lappe	06/09/1918	14/09/1918
War Diary	In The Line	15/09/1918	21/09/1918
War Diary	Abeele	22/09/1918	27/09/1918
War Diary	Lappe	28/09/1918	28/09/1918
War Diary	Verbranden Molen	29/09/1918	30/09/1918
War Diary		04/09/1918	04/09/1918
Miscellaneous	The Secretary Kent F.F. Assen. Maidstone.	25/09/1918	25/09/1918
Miscellaneous	Officer Commanding 15th Bat. Hampshire Regt.	05/11/1917	05/11/1917
War Diary		01/10/1918	06/10/1918
War Diary	Hoograaf	07/10/1918	31/10/1918
War Diary		19/10/1918	26/10/1918
War Diary		02/10/1918	26/10/1918
Miscellaneous	Headquarters. 122nd. Infantry Brigade.	03/12/1918	03/12/1918
War Diary		01/11/1918	11/11/1918
War Diary	Nukerke	12/11/1918	14/11/1918

War Diary	Paricke	15/11/1918	18/11/1918
War Diary	Bievene	19/11/1918	20/11/1918
War Diary	Goefferdingen	21/11/1918	30/11/1918
Heading	Casualties for November 1918	05/11/1918	22/11/1918
War Diary	Goefferdinghe	01/12/1918	11/12/1918
War Diary	Coquaine	12/12/1918	12/12/1918
War Diary	Saintes	13/12/1918	13/12/1918
War Diary	Wauthier-Braine	14/12/1918	15/12/1918
War Diary	Vieux-Genappe	16/12/1918	16/12/1918
War Diary	Villers-La-Ville	17/12/1918	17/12/1918
War Diary	Sambreffe	18/12/1918	18/12/1918
War Diary	St. Servais	19/12/1918	19/12/1918
War Diary	Waret-L'Eveque	20/12/1918	20/12/1918
War Diary	Vieux-et-Borset	21/12/1918	31/12/1918
War Diary		02/12/1918	12/12/1918
Heading	15th Bn Hampshire Regt Jan-Mar 1919		
War Diary	Vieux Et Borset	01/01/1919	08/01/1919
War Diary	Overath	09/01/1919	24/02/1919
War Diary	Marialinden	25/02/1919	22/03/1919
War Diary	Hoffnungstall	23/03/1919	24/03/1919
War Diary	Opladen	24/03/1919	24/03/1919
War Diary	Leichlingen	25/03/1919	26/03/1919
War Diary	Wermelskirchen	27/03/1919	31/03/1919

WD 95/2634(6)

WD45/2634(6)

122nd Inf.Bde.
41st Div.

Battn. returned with
Bde. to France from
Italy 1/5.3.18.

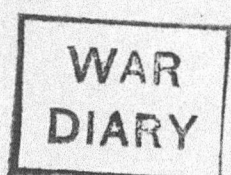

15th BATTN. THE HAMPSHIRE REGIMENT.

M A R C H

1 9 1 8

WAR DIARY
or
INTELLIGENCE SUMMARY.

(Erase heading not required.)

Army Form C. 2118.

15th Bn. Hampshire Regt.

Place	Date	Hour	Summary of Events and Information	Remarks and references to Appendices
S. MARTINO	1/3/18		Right half Battalion marched to CARMIGNANO to entrain for France	
"	2/3/18		Left half Battalion do. do.	
"	3/3/18		In the train	
France	4/3/18			
WARLINCOURT	5/3/18		Right half Battalion detrained at MONDICOURT and marched to Billets at WARLINCOURT arriving in billets at 2.30 p.m. Left half. Battalion did likewise arriving at WARLINCOURT at 1 A.M.	
"	6/3/18		Day spent in cleaning up, inspections under company arrangements	
"	7/3/18		Training under company arrangements from 8.30 a.m - 1 p.m	
"	8/3/18		Training under company arrangements 8.30 a.m - 2 p.m	

Army Form C. 2118.

WAR DIARY
or
INTELLIGENCE SUMMARY.
(Erase heading not required.)

Instructions regarding War Diaries and Intelligence Summaries are contained in F. S. Regs., Part II. and the Staff Manual respectively. Title pages will be prepared in manuscript.

Place	Date	Hour	Summary of Events and Information	Remarks and references to Appendices
WARLINCOURT	9/3/18		Church parades.	
"	10/3/18		Battalion route march WARLINCOURT – PAS – AUTIENE – TIEVRES – PAS Baths in afternoon	
"	11/3/18		Training under company arrangements 8.30am – 4.pm.	
"	12/3/18		Tactical exercise by Battalion two D Coy Specialist training D Coy 8.30 – 11.30 range at MONDICOURT 12 noon – 5pm	
"	13/3/18		Training as per programme 8.30am – 3pm Baths	
"	14/3/18		" 8.30am – 10pm	
"	15/3/18		10am Route march. Battalion MONDICOURT – PAS – WARLINCOURT Coy training as per programme – range at MONDICOURT 8.30am – 10am – Battalion rev	
"	14/3/18		march	
"	16/3/18		Church parades – Baths	

WAR DIARY
or
INTELLIGENCE SUMMARY.
(Erase heading not required.)

Army Form C. 2118.

Place	Date	Hour	Summary of Events and Information	Remarks and references to Appendices
WARLINCOURT	17		Coy Training as per program. Conference misted models of both fronts at Brigade H.Q.	
"	18.		Coy Training as per program 8.30 AM – 4 PM.	
	19.		do. do. – 5 PM. range at MONDICOURT allotted	
	20.		do. do. to coys. do. do.	
	21.		Battalion left WARLINCOURT & entrained for RIBEMONT area, but owing to the enemy attack Battn. detrained at ACHIET-LE-GRAND & marched to SAVOY CAMP & stopped for the night.	
ACHIET-LE-GRAND	22	1 P.M.	Battn. left SAVOY CAMP at 1 PM & marched in fighting order to assembly position at WATER POINT on BAPAUME – SAPIGNIES ROAD when it halted in artillery formation	
		6 P.M.	Battn. was ordered to take up a position & dig in facing BUGNATRE relief was complete by midnight 22/23 with C & D Coys in front line & A Suffolks B in Reserve	
	22/23			
	23	1 AM	The 18th East Surreys who were on our right were ordered to take up a line facing MORY on our left. The Battn. had to spread out & put in touch with 18th K.R.R. on our right. This was slow & done in daylight.	
		7 AM	Battn. ordered to take up a position in support of 12th E. Surreys facing MORY.	

Army Form C. 2118.

WAR DIARY
or
INTELLIGENCE SUMMARY.
(Erase heading not required.)

Instructions regarding War Diaries and Intelligence Summaries are contained in F. S. Regs., Part II. and the Staff Manual respectively. Title pages will be prepared in manuscript.

Place	Date	Hour	Summary of Events and Information	Remarks and references to Appendices
Contd:	23rd		with two Coys in Brigade Reserve	
		11AM	The two Coys in Brigade Reserve took up a position in front line on its L of MORY. The 13th MDDX were on the left & 10/11th H.L.I. on its right. During the day C. Coy suffered casualties from hostile shell fire 14 killed 30 wounded	
	24th	11PM	Enemy attack in face & Battn. Repulsed the enemy with heavy losses. Casualties enemy light.	
	25th	11PM	Enemy attacked in face & on right of Battn. Held position until enemy (24.00) were N & S of position when Bn was relieved to retire. During the retirement 2 prisoners were taken, who informed us that enemy were on both flanks.	advancing
	26th	4AM.	New Battn. took up a position facing E, & waited till dawn to see w of BIHUCOURT WOOD	
		11AM.	w/ye troops in an immediate front retired on to an line & the enemy attacked. In its hollow in our rear were a Brigade of the MANCHESTERS & on the enemy advancing turned on left flank. A message was sent to OC MANCHESTERS informing them of the situation & asking what assistance he was going to render.	

WAR DIARY or INTELLIGENCE SUMMARY

Army Form C. 2118.

Place	Date	Hour	Summary of Events and Information	Remarks and references to Appendices
(Continued)	26th		The orderly who was despatched with the message returned & to Bde Brigade who demanded "One Coy", & despatched one Battn to our right flank & another to our left to support. One Coy being closely moved up in the centre of our line.	
		1 P.M.	Situation very serious as the enemy was massing in BIHUCOURT WOOD.	
		2 P.M.	Three TANKS advanced over our front & 8 on our right flank, all did extraordinary good work & after being in the enemy lines for an hour returned to our lines when two of them were knocked out. All endeavours were made to inform the O.C. of moving tank they were urgently required to force through BIHUCOURT WOOD without success. The enemy dug in on ridge opposite our front & the situation greatest alarm.	
		3 P.M.		
		12. midnight	Situation extraordinary quiet. The line was now held as follows: one Coy of 12th E. Surreys, on our immediate right & our Battn of Manchesters on their right. One Coy Manchester in centre & C. Coy & one Battn of Manchesters distributed in support.	
27th		1 A.M.	All troops in the line received orders to withdraw commencing from the right B. C. & D. Coys withdrew without molestation. A. Coy	

WAR DIARY
or
INTELLIGENCE SUMMARY.
(Erase heading not required).

Army Form C. 2118.

Place	Date	Hour	Summary of Events and Information	Remarks and references to Appendices
Cold.	27th		the Left Coy in the line was about to withdraw its enemy attacked supported with strong machine gun barrage. his attacked in force. A Coy withdrew fighting a brilliant rear guard action. Casualties received on 26th inst. 18. 27th inst. Battn HQrs B & D Coys arrived at Bucquoy at 6 AM. to find A & C Coy. there after this have sat in the area of Bucquoy. Battn marched to took up a position E. of GOMMECOURT.	
		12 P.M.	BATTN received orders to proceed to BIEN— FONCVILLERS. arriving there 2 AM 28th Jan'ry the men in an open field	
BIENVILLERS au Bois	28th	11 AM	The Battn moved into BIENVILLERS Wood along side of ACHESON A. the remainder of Div in same vicinity.	
	29th	11 AM	BATTN returned to the position E. of GOMMECOURT in support to the 63rd Div. The line was held with A.B & D Coys. in front. the C. in support.	
		6 P.M.	Orders were received for an Coy to attack NOSSIGNAL WOOD & to fill up the gap between 63rd DIV & 4th AUSTRALIAN Bde.	

WAR DIARY
or
INTELLIGENCE SUMMARY.
(Erase heading not required.)

Army Form C. 2118.

Place	Date	Hour	Summary of Events and Information	Remarks and references to Appendices
		6.15 PM	These orders were cancelled.	
		6.25 PM	These orders were again given.	
		6.35 PM	Orders were again cancelled on the intention now to return to our Coy to clean up	
		6.45 PM	Orders were again given to attack + A. Coy. were detailed to carry out this operation. It was arranged for a fighting patrol to go out + reconnoitre NAMELESS FARM which we found afterwards to be occupied by about 200 of the enemy about the time	
		11.PM	when A. Coy. were kind up in the mean COMMECOURT – HEBITURNE Road, + were advancing the attack when an unexpectedly counter order was received to abandon the attack which was eventually complied with, to the satisfaction of all. The night was foggy with rain + mist, could not have been worse. Patrols went out 1 prisoner taken.	
	30th		Battn remained in the same positions Casualties 2.	

WAR DIARY
or
INTELLIGENCE SUMMARY.
(Erase heading not required.)

Army Form C. 2118.

Place	Date	Hour	Summary of Events and Information	Remarks and references to Appendices
	31st	2AM	Battn was relieved by 5th 7th Manchesters @ 3AM.	
		5AM	Battn relieved the 6th part of 7th Manchesters in support in a position N.E. of ESSART.	
			Casualties for month.	
			Officers 4 wounded.	
			16 OR Killed.	
			61 Wounded	
			5 missing.	

41st Division.
122nd Infantry Brigade

WAR DIARY

15th BATTALION

THE HAMPSHIRE REGIMENT

APRIL 1918

From:
    Officer Commanding,
        15th. Batt. Hampshire Regt.

To:
    Headquarters,
        122nd. Infantry Brigade.

L.R. 945

        Herewith WAR DIARY for the month of April 1918.

2/4/18.

                      Lieut. Colonel.
        Commanding 15th. Batt. Hampshire Regiment.

15TH
(S) BATTALION,
THE HAMPSHIRE REGT.

No ....
Date ....

WAR DIARY
or
INTELLIGENCE SUMMARY.
(Erase heading not required.)

Instructions regarding War Diaries and Intelligence Summaries are contained in F. S. Regs., Part II. and the Staff Manual respectively. Title pages will be prepared in manuscript.

Army Form C. 2118.

Place	Date	Hour	Summary of Events and Information	Remarks and references to Appendices
ESSARTS	1/4/18		Battalion was relieved by 6th Manchester Regt and entrained by 11.30 P.M. battalion embussed for MARIEUX aerodrome where it stayed the night	
MARIEUX	2/4/18		Battalion marched from the aerodrome at 2.30 P.M. to billets in ORVILLE where it remained till the following day	
ORVILLE	3/4/18		Battalion paraded at 8.30 A.M. and marched to a halt on the MARIEUX – AUTHIE road where it embussed for FREVENT it then rested in a field and entrained at 9.30 P.M. for POPERINGHE.	
POPERINGHE	4/4/18		Battalion detrained in the vicinity, marched into the town arriving at billets here at 8.30 A.M. – Battalion rested till 4.30 P.M. when it marched to SCHOOL CAMP where it remained till the afternoon of 7th	

WAR DIARY
or
INTELLIGENCE SUMMARY.
(Erase heading not required.)

Army Form C. 2118.

Place	Date	Hour	Summary of Events and Information	Remarks and references to Appendices
SCHOOL CAMP	5/4/18		Day spent in clearing and replacing deficiencies as far as possible - Inspections under company arrangements	
SCHOOL CAMP	6/4/18		The Battalion was paraded for inspection by General Sir H.C.O. PLUMER G.C.B., G.C.M.G., G.C.V.O., A.D.C. who was unable to attend. Battalion was inspected by Lt. General Sir A. Hunter-Weston K.C.M.G. Major-General to S. Rawlinson Bart and Special Orders of the day were <del>read out to the men by me</del> on <del>behalf</del> of the <del>enemy offensive</del>.	
SCHOOL CAMP	7/4/18		Battalion left camp in two parties, entrained and proceeded to OPERINGHE where they entrained for IBERIAN (Light Railway) and marched up to relieve the 1st Lancashire Fusiliers in the PASSENDAELE sector C+D Coys in the line A+B in support - relief successfully accomplished by 11.30 P.M.	
PASSENDAELE sector	8/4/18		Situation normal. casualties nil	

Army Form C. 2118.

WAR DIARY
or
INTELLIGENCE SUMMARY.
(Erase heading not required.)

Place	Date	Hour	Summary of Events and Information	Remarks and references to Appendices
PASSENDAELE sector	9/4/18		Situation normal – casualties nil. Two patrols were sent out to reconnoitre battalion front, no enemy were encountered or heard	
"	10/4/18		Situation normal – casualties nil. Two patrols were again sent out – but owing to the extreme darkness progress was very difficult, a machine gun post was however located at the GASOMETERS E.9.a.8.8. Marked artillery activity on our right.	
"	11/4/18		Situation critical owing to enemy advance on our right, a retirement thought probable and plans made to cope with same – however a counterattack in which our troops took part some of the lost ground restored our position two anxious ... Battalion relieved 1/5 South Staffords relief completed by 12 midnight Battalion proceeded to huts/tents at Irish Farm. Casualties during tour – nil.	

Army Form C. 2118.

WAR DIARY
or
INTELLIGENCE SUMMARY.
(Erase heading not required.)

Instructions regarding War Diaries and Intelligence Summaries are contained in F. S. Regs., Part II. and the Staff Manual respectively. Title pages will be prepared in manuscript.

Place	Date	Hour	Summary of Events and Information	Remarks and references to Appendices
PASSCHENDAELE	12/4/18		Battalion rested in hutments till 5P.M. when it marched up to relieve the 5th S. Stafford's and 7th N. Stafford's taking over the left brigade sector in the form of an out post to cover the withdrawal from the PASSCHENDAELE salient. relief complete 11.30 P.M casualties nil.	
"	13/4/18		situation normal casualties one frequent patrols were sent out from each company front no enemy were encountered.	
"	14/4/18		situation normal casualties nil patrols as for the 13th Enst. nothing to report.	
"	15/4/18		situation normal casualties nil - patrols report that enemy very light officer nearer.	
"	16/4/18		Battalion withdrew from the salient at 3 A.M; each company till a line a little further under an officer to	

WAR DIARY
or
INTELLIGENCE SUMMARY.
(Erase heading not required.)

Army Form C. 2118.

Place	Date	Hour	Summary of Events and Information	Remarks and references to Appendices
PASSCHENDAELE	10/4/18		soon it withdrawal. The enemy were apparently ignorant of the day of our withdrawal, although his prisoners stated he was aware that we contemplated falling back. Although his shelling was normal the company in PASSCHENDAELE state that enemy lights appeared to follow them as they withdrew. The battalion arrived without incident at their alloted camp (PENLLELI), the last company arriving at 9AM. Casualties during the tour one O.R. A meal was provided for the men on arrival after which they rested the remainder of the day	
YPRES.	11/4/18		Battalion was employed in reclaiming a line of trenches in the vicinity of the camp, each company working eight hours	

Army Form C. 2118.

WAR DIARY
or
INTELLIGENCE SUMMARY.
(Erase heading not required.)

Instructions regarding War Diaries and Intelligence Summaries are contained in F.S. Regs., Part II. and the Staff Manual respectively. Title pages will be prepared in manuscript.

Place	Date	Hour	Summary of Events and Information	Remarks and references to Appendices
18/4/18 YPRES.				
	19/4/18		The battalion was employed retaining trenches and wiring same.	
			As for 18/4/18. The Brigade being so reduced in not only its own division but also the 9th & 36th divisions was reconnoitring parties were sent to find the best route & called upon to support the former division.	
"	20/4/18		Working parties as before. YPRES was shelled nearly with gas shells during the night but the Battalion camp being situated about 1 mile N.W. was not affected	
"	21/4/18		Working parties as before. YPRES again received attention during the night and heavy firing was heard from the direction of Mt KEMMEL. Enemy aircraft were active but no bombs fell in the camp	

Army Form C. 2118.

WAR DIARY
or
INTELLIGENCE SUMMARY.
(Erase heading not required.)

Instructions regarding War Diaries and Intelligence Summaries are contained in F. S. Regs., Part II. and the Staff Manual respectively. Title pages will be prepared in manuscript.

Place	Date	Hour	Summary of Events and Information	Remarks and references to Appendices
YPRES	22/4/18		Working parties as previously took production very satisfactory - parties were again sent out of reconnoitre routes & assembly points.	
"	23/4/18		Working parties the same except one company was sent to work in the forward area, other companies worked 6 hours.	
"	24/4/18		Working parties as for 23/4/18, a note of appreciation for the fine work done by the battalion in reclaiming the trenches was received from the divisional commander. Parties reconnoitred the routes to, and assembly point behind the 36th divisional front in the event of the brigade being called upon to counter attack in this area. Enemy aircraft was active during the night and numerous bombs were dropped in the vicinity, none fell in the camp.	

Army Form C. 2118

WAR DIARY
or
INTELLIGENCE SUMMARY
(Erase heading not required.)

Place	Date	Hour	Summary of Events and Information	Remarks and references to Appendices
YPRES	24/4/18		Working parties as usual. A violent bombardment started at 3 A.M. in the vicinity of Mt KEMMEL which lasted till 8.30 A.M. Enemy artillery was active during the morning shelling roads & heavy batteries round YPRES.	
"	25/4/18		At 9.15 A.M. orders were received to be prepared to move at 2 hours notice, working parties ceased work. Artillery was again active in the direction of Mt KEMMEL but not so violent as the preceding day. Hostile artillery fairly active round YPRES. Battalion still under notice to move on half. orders	
"	26/4/18		at 11.30 P.M. orders were received forced to brigade assembly point 28 N.W. H.5.d.55. Battalion remained at this point in company groups till 6.30 P.M. when orders were received to proceed to ORILLIA CAMP B.26.C.7.2. Enemy aircraft was active at low altitudes during the days	

WAR DIARY
or
INTELLIGENCE SUMMARY

(Erase heading not required.)

Army Form C. 2118

Place	Date	Hour	Summary of Events and Information	Remarks and references to Appendices
ORILLIA CAMP	27/4/18		Battalion stood down notice to move being two hours day spent in cleaning up and inspections under company arrangements.	
"	28/4/18		Day was spent in Gas Drill and Specialist training notice received that 12th Brigade would relieve 11th Brigade on night of 28/29th. This was cancelled as the order being received to 'stand-to' training ceased at 11am. being ready artillery firing in direction of Mt KEMMEL. Battalion stood down to two hour notice at 6 P.M. General and Specialist training.	
"	29/4/18			
"	30/4/18		Training as for 29/4/18 orders received that 12th Brigade would probably relieve 11th Brigade on night of 2nd/3rd May. Casualties for April. 1 O.R. wounded.	

From:- Officer Commanding,
　　15th Batt. Hampshire Regiment,
To :- Headquarters,
　　122nd Infantry Brigade.

L.R. 205

Herewith War Diary for the month of May 1918.

Clive Murdoch Lieut.-Colonel,
Commanding 15th (S.) Batln. Hampshire Regt.

3rd June 1918.

WAR DIARY. — 15th Hampshire Regt.

May 1st	Second Anniversary of the 15th Hampshire Regt's arrival in France. All N.C.O.s & men who took part were addressed on parade by the C.O. at 11.0 am. General & Specialist Training. Draft 7 O.R.	
2nd	Battalion left ORILLA camp to relieve 20th D.L.I. In YPRES RAMPARTS Left sub-sector, in the following order from right to left — A, B, D, C. 18 K.R.R's on right – 36th D.N. on left.	Sheet 28 N.W.
3rd	Working & salvage parties supplied. Also work on YPRES DEFENCES.	
4th	"	
5th	"	
6th	" Draft 3 N.C.O's. 6 O.R.	
7th	Battalion relieved 12th E. Surrey Regt in right sub sector outpost line (S. of POTIZE) A & B Coys in front line, C in support, D in reserve in RAMPARTS. Batt HQ – I 9 a 15.80	
8th	"	
9th	"	
10th	Redistribution of Coys. – A Coy took over 80 yds of front line to left, B Coy sidestepped to left & two Coys 18th K.R.R.C. came on front line on the right.	
11th	C Coy moved up two rear platoons from reserve to support line, & D Coy occupied reserve line with 3 platoons.	
12th		
13th	2 Platoons of A, C & D of B Coy relieved by 3 platoons of C Coy & the three companies arranged in depth.	
14th		
15th		
17th	Battalion was relieved by 10th R.W. Kent Regt & marched to ORILLA camp.	
18th	Rest in camp. Baths. Draft 1 N.C.O. 34 O.R.	

WAR DIARY

May 19th	Working parties on VLAMERTINGHE defences.	Draft. 5. O.R.
20th	" "	Draft 10. O.R.
21st	" "	Draft. 1 N.CO 11. O.R
22nd	Coy. & Specialist training	" 1 N.CO 6. O.R
23rd	Coy & Specialist training	
24th	Brigadiers inspection cancelled by rain. Training in afternoon.	
25th	Parade & inspection by G.O.C. 122. Inf. Bde., Presentation of medal ribbons & address to all who did patrols in the sector. Draft 1 N.CO 4. O.R.	
26th	Battalion relieved 20th D.L.I. in support to right Batt. Brigade sector. C Coy in DOLL'S HOUSE LINE, D Coy – LAUNDRY, – B & B. E & F GOLDFISH CHATEAU.	
26th 27th 28th 29th 30th 31st	Work on Coy. positions & alternative positions to a flank & salvage work: Sector very quiet except for slight H.E. & gas shelling of rear positions. Casualties during the tour Officer Ranks. Killed – 2. Wounded 8 – Gassed – 8 –	

May. 1918.

WAR DIARY — APPENDIX I.

HONOURS AND AWARDS during MAY.—

D.S.O. — Lt Col. C. Murdoch.

Bar to M.C. — Capt. S.H. Wigmore M.C.
Bar to M.C. — Capt. C.C. Oxtoroto M.C.
M.C. — Capt. C.C. Newman
" — Lieut E.M. Trevett.
" — 2 Lieut S.M. Shadlock
M.C. — Lt. J.T. Spencer.
(whilst with 14th Hants)

Military Medal.—

204767	Pte	Goodchild W.G.
204701	"	Beunken S.G.
201855	"	Gladwell J.E.
26760	Serg	Ware A.
264560	Pte	Pitts F.J.
209813	"	Matcham H.
26607	L.C.	Denny N.W.
28107	Cpl.	Hampton W.
204990	Pte	Burden H.C.
297182	"	King H.J.
29817	"	Priess E.C.
27315	Cpl.	Pellett G.
242811	Pte	Aslam H.
23158	Serg	H.H Edward
26501	L.C.	Deane E.D.
257312	Pte	Silvester J.

D.C.M.s
26960 — Serg Falconer G.
Bar to D.C.M.
No. 8040 Serg Newton G.

CASUALTIES MAY 1918.

WOUNDED — 2 Lieut E.M. Sandell. — May 12th

O.R.s
KILLED 4
WOUNDED 25
DIED FROM GAS 1
GASSED 14
 Total — 45.

OFFICERS JOINED during MAY.

Lieut P.N. Boosted M.C.   2/Lt. G.H. Seal
2 Lieut D.E. Carley   Lt. G.D. Weddeburn
  "   R.G. Sutton A.S.   2/Lt. O.H. Brown
Capt. J.H. Gunner
2 Lieut. F.J.N. Vincent
Lieut J.L. Spencer M.C. (Rejoining).

Olive Murdoch
Lieut.-Colonel,
Commanding 15th (S.) Batt. Hampshire Regt.

WAR DIARY 15 Hampshire

June		
1	YPRES	Battalion in reserve line usual working parties no casualties
2	"	do do Reinforcements 13 ORs
3	"	do do do
		Orders received that division would be relieved by 49 Division. Battalion was relieved by 7th Duke of Wellington Regt. Relief complete by 11 pm casualties nil
4	PROVEN	Battalion entrained at PROVEN at 7.30 pm and proceeded by tactical train to WATTEN and marched to OUEST-MOUNT
5	OUEST-MOUNT	Battalion arrived at 1.30 am day spent on rest and cleaning up. reinforcements 2 ORs.
6	"	Company and specialist training – range. reinforcements 13 ORs. Battalion on the range reinforcements 1 officer 8 ORs.
7	"	Coy and specialist training – Baths
8	"	Sunday – church parade – rest
9	"	Coy and specialist training
10	"	Coy and specialist training – firing on range with Lewis guns.
11	"	do do
12	"	do do
13	"	do do
14	"	do do
15	"	do do
16		Church parade – rest

WAR DIARY

15TH (S) BATT.
HAMPSHIRE REGT.
No..........
Date..........

	JUNE	
JUNE 17	OUESTMOUNT	Company and specialist training
18	"	Bullet and Bayonet competition.
19	"	Battalion scheme.
20	"	Brigade scheme
21	"	Battalion on the range. Battalion concert
22	"	Company and specialist training has test at Brigade H.Q.
23	"	Church parade and rest
24	"	Company and specialist training - Baths
25	"	Battalion marched to RUPROUCK area - no men fell out distance 15 miles
26	WATOU	Battalion marched to WATOU area and took over billets vacated by XV French Corps - no men fell out distance 17 miles
27	"	Battalion rested.
28	"	Company + specialist training, parties visited sects to be taken over from the French.
29	REMY	Battalion marched to ABEELE where it bivouacced for the night near Canadian C.C.S., REMY.
30	LA CLYTTE	Battalion relieved 1st Battalion 103rd Regt French Army in front line. Left Bde sector (in front of LA CLYTTE) Battn HQ - MURRUMBIDGEE CAMP - March from REMY commenced at 9.0 pm Relief complete 2.0 am. See Appendix Casualties 7

WO95/2631

JUNE 1918. WAR DIARY. APPENDIX.

HONOURS & AWARDS – June 1918.

Birthday Honours.

The Military Cross – Capt. P.E. Leybourne.
The D.C.M. – No.18024. C.S.M. Collis F.C. M.M.
The M.S.M. – 20209. R.S.M. Greenwood F. M.C.
" – 17579. R.Q.M.S. Tragus. H.

Mentioned in Dispatches. 18.4.18

Capt. S.H. Wigmore M.C.
2/Lieut G.A. Betttinson – (Att 122 T.M.B.)
22963. Serj. Evans J.
20903. " Lonergan J.J.
7399 " Stone. H. M.M.
18700. L.Corp. Munslow F. M.M.

CASUALTIES. June 1918

KILLED IN ACTION :-

10911. Pte Winter A. – (A Coy) 1.6.18
.8461. C.S.M. Nunn J DCM (D Coy) 30.6.18
204802. Pte Lunter W " " "
39141 " Noyce H " " "

WOUNDED

18665 Pte Williams H (B Coy) 1.6.18
235017 " Lee. W.H " " "
24555 " Smith. J. " " "
204804 " Lemon F. " 30.6.18
209702 " Bienvenue " (D Coy) " "
204767 " Gottchild W. " " "
204491 " Bates. A. " " "
204837 " Halloway W. " " "

ROLL OF OFFICERS WITH BATTALION 30.6.18

Lt. Col Clive Murdoch. D.S.O. [Leave U.K.]
Major A.W. Puttick. M.C.
Capt. & Adj. F.H. Wigmore. M.C.
Capt. J.A. Mowat. M.C. Transport officer.
Lieut. F.J. Whaley M.C. A/Intelligence officer

Capt. C.C. Oxtonow. M.C.
Lieut J.L. Spencer. M.C.
Lieut. P.C. Elliot
Lieut. P.J.N. Vincent
2 Lieut. F.H. Damp
2 Lieut. C. Kneebone.

Capt. P.E. Leybourne. M.C.
2 Lieut. G.H. Seal
" A.A. Bradlow
" O.A. Brown

Capt. J.P. Fowler. M.C.
Lieut. H.M. Tollemache
2 Lieut. G.J. Potter
2 Lieut F.W. Lee

Capt. C.C. Newman M.C.
Capt. J.A.E. Long
2 Lieut K. Graham
" S.C. Satch
" A.W. White

15TH (S) BATT.
HAMPSHIRE REGT.

WAR DIARY. — JULY 1918 — 15th(S) Batn THE HAMPSHIRE REGT

LA CLYTTE SECTOR	1st July	Relief of French troops completed. French stores etc removed by regimental transport.
	2nd	
	3rd	
	4th	
	5th	Battalion relieved in front line by 12th E Surrey Regt, and took over support line from 16th K.R.R.C. Two Coys on each side of LA CLYTTE–RENINGHELST road.
	6th	Working parties supplied nightly for digging & wiring LA CLYTTE defences. —
	7th	
	8th	
	9th	
	10th	Battalion relieved in reserve support line by 12th E Surrey Regt. & took over reserve line from 16th K.R.R.C. Companies in huts & dugouts along the WESTOUTRE line near ZEVECOTEN.
	11th	Working parties supplied for WESTOUTRE line & buried cable by night and small parties by day. Companies march to baths near WIPPEN HOEK.
	12th	
	13th	
	14th	
	15th	Battalion took over front line from 18 K.R.R.C. C Coy in front line, D, A, & B in LA CLYTTE line. Officers & NCO's of American army attached for instruction

Clive Hunter-Loudy
Lieut Col.
Comdg. 15th Hampshire Regt

WAR DIARY. July 1918. 15th (S) Batn The HAMPSHIRE Regt -

LA CLYTTE Sector	July 16th	Patrols reconnoitred ground for intended raid.
	17th	Bombing encounter between patrol of D Coy under 2 Lieut WHITE & enemy post at KIM CAMP. Four of patrol wounded but all carried back to our lines. Heavy shelling in the early morning & S.O.S from Bde on right. Lt H.M. Hollemagle killed
	18th	Heavy counter preparation by our artillery.
	19th	Our patrols very active
	20th	Battalion relieved by 12th E Surrey Regt, & returned to supports relieving 18 K.R.R.L.
	21st	Working parties as usual by night
	22.	Parties sent to ground line to reconnoitre for raid.
	23.	A raid was carried out by one platoon of A & one of D Coys on enemy line of the KLEINE KEMMELBECK. (See B.O.O. no 122) Objective was gained in the centre, but flanks were held up by M.G. fire. No prisoners were taken, but about 4 enemy killed. Our casualties 2 killed, 4 wounded Officers in charge were 2/Lieuts C. Kneebone & F.W. Lee
	24.	Battalion engaged in night working parties as usual
	25.	The Battalion was relieved by 12 E Surreys & went into reserve in WESTOUTRE line.
	26.	
	27.	
	28.	
	29.	
	30.	Three Coys of the Battalion relieved 3 Coys of 12th E Surreys in the

Nine hundred
Lieut-Col.
Comdg. 15th Hampshire Regt.

WAR DIARY. July 1918. 15th (S) Batn. The HAMPSHIRE Regt.

LA CLYTTE SECTOR	July 30th (cont.)	on the LA CLYTTE line, the front line being held by 1 Coy. 106th Regt U.S.A. A Coy remained in reserve area at QUEBEC camp. Heavy enemy counter-preparation 2-0-30. AM
	July 31st	A Coy relieved Americans in front line. Guides arrived to Coys from 4th Canadian Mounted Rifles.
		— APPENDIX —
		Casualties during the month of July —
		KILLED — 1 Officer — (Lt H.M. Tollemache) 1 W.O (C.S.M J. NUNN. D.C.M) 12 Other Ranks —
		WOUNDED — 1 Officer — (Lt J.L Shincer M.C (remained at duty). 53 Other Ranks. 1 Other rank wounded & remained at duty.
		MISSING — 2 Other Ranks
		Total Casualties for the month :- 70.

Clive Murdoch
Lieut. Col.
Comdg. 15th Hampshire Regt.

SECRET.   Copy No. 8

Battalion Operation Order No. 122 by Lieut-Colonel C. MURDOCH, D.S.O.
Commanding "BRANCH".
Dated 22nd July 1918.

Reference Map.   Sheet 28 S.W.

1. A raid will be carried out by One platoon of "A" Company and One platoon of "D" Company on night 23rd/24th July, 1918.

2. It is intended that raiding party should penetrate enemy's position to obtain:-
    a. An identification.
    b. To capture a live prisoner.
    c. To obtain information re hostile trench mortar emplacement.

3. The objective of the party will be the Railway line running from N 14 d 05 76 to N 14 b 35 35 enemy outpost line.
    On arriving at objective each platoon will work along enemy's defences towards N 14 b 20 08.
    The right hand section of "A" Coy platoon will advance direct for bridge leading over the KLEINE-KEMMEL BEEK at N 14 b 35 10, to endeavour to prevent the enemy from retreating by that bridge.

4. Each platoon detailed to carry out raid will consist of 1 Officer, 1 Sergt and 4 sections each of 1 N.C.O. and 6 men.
    The Officer for "A" Coy platoon will be 2/Lieut C. KNEEBONE and for "D" Coy 2/Lieut F.W. LEE.
    These platoons will consist of one section taken from each platoon in the Company.

5. Zero hour to be notified later, probably at 1-30 a.m. 24th July.

6. "A" Coy's platoon will be formed up in front of our wire with right flank at N 14 b 13 58 on a tape laid on a true bearing of 56°.
    "D" Coy's platoon will be formed up in front of our wire with right flank at N 14 a 80 12 on a tape laid on a true bearing of 50°.
    Tapes will be laid out about 100 ft in front of our wire on above lines to mark the jumping off places, by the Platoon Commanders of the raiding platoons on night 23/24th inst to be in position two hours before Zero.
    A covering party of 1 N.C.O. and 10 men will be found by the 12th East Surrey Regt for each party laying out these tapes. These covering parties will also act as covering party for platoons when assembling.
    They must be prepared to keep any of the enemy's patrols off the raiding party until Zero hour, when they will withdraw to trench.
    Assembling troops will be in position half an hour before Zero.

7. Platoons will assemble on the tapes in line of sections in file, section Commanders in front of their sections, platoon commanders in front of their platoons, platoon Sergts in rear of platoons.
    5 minutes before Zero hour platoon commanders will notify section commanders of the time.
    At Zero hour the platoons will advance rapidly, sections led by the section commanders to the gaps in the wire, previously located.
    When the raiding party have got through the enemy's wire they will shout and make as much noise as possible.

8. True bearing of Attack:-
    "A" Coy's platoon 145° True bearing.
    "D" Coy's platoon 140° True bearing.

9. Watches will be synchronised on the telephone between Battalion and Company H.Q. at 10-45 p.m. 23rd inst.
    The Officers in charge of the attacking platoons will be at Front Line Coy's H.Q. (12th East Surrey Regt) at that hour.
    The attack of the two platoons must be simultaneous.

10. Equipment.   As light as possible.
    Steel Helmets will be worn and Box Respirators will be carried.
    Rifles loaded with 10 rounds and Bayonets blackened.
    10 rounds of S.A.A. in pocket.
    No other equipment.
    Only N.C.Os. will carry 2 bombs to be used in an emergency only, and an electric torch.
    Officers and Platoon Sergts will carry a Very Light Pistol and 6 1" GREEN Very Lights for the purpose of giving the recall signal.

Officers and/

(2)

10. continued.
Officers and Platoon Sergts will be sure to have a luminous watch which must be kept covered.
Company Commanders concerned are held responsible that all shoulder straps, pay books and identification are taken off men before assault.

11. 12th East Surrey Regt will supply two Lewis Gun teams to crawl out with Lewis Guns in NO MANS LAND up to our wire (i.e. if it will improve their field of fire, otherwise they will remain in trench) so as to be in position by Zero hour at each of the following points ready to fire at any hostile machine gun which opens fire at the raiding party:-
    One Lewis Gun at N 14 a 70 05.
    " " " " N 14 b 30 60.
All Lewis Guns in the front line will be ready at Zero hour to fire at any hostile machine gun which opens fire, but no gun must fire over the ground in which the raid is being made until Zero plus 25 minutes.

12. When the raiding party has succeeded in taking some prisoners or have been in the enemy's position 10 minutes the Platoon Officer will fire a GREEN Very Light on which signal raiding party will return to our trenches.
If this signal has not been fired in 15 minutes the platoon Sergts will fire the withdrawal signal.
Lieut J.L. SPENCER, who will be at N 14 b 25 60 and 2/Lieut H.W. GREEN who will be at N 14 a 70 18 will fire a RED Very Light into the ground on the parapet 10 minutes after Zero hour to give the direction to the returning raiding party and continue firing at their own discretion.
On returning to our Front Line trenches each man in a section is responsible that the whole of the section are present.
When sections have assembled in front line trenches they will proceed to Front Line Coy H.Q. at N 7 d 6 6
When platoon commanders are satisfied that the whole of their platoons are all present they will report to Lieut P.N. BOUSTEAD M.C. at Front Line Coy, H.Q. who will in turn wire Battalion H.Q.
After Platoons have assembled at Front Line Coy H.Q. they will proceed to Battalion H.Q.
All men must be shown Front Line Coy H.Q. tonight.

13. PASS WORD.
In view of the possibility of the raiding parties meeting and not recognising each other the pass word "MURDOCH" will be adopted.
If two of the raiding parties meet in the enemy's defences and there is any suspicion that one of them is an enemy the pass word will be immediately shouted out and if the adversary does not immediately answer by shouting the pass word, it will be taken that he is one of the enemy.

14. ARTILLERY.
The enemy's front line in the vicinity of N 19 a (124th I.B. Front) will be heavily barraged at Zero hour.
The Machine Gun nest at N 14 b 7 9 will be engaged with Stokes Mortars from Zero hour onwards.
A protective barrage to enable the raiding party to return to our trenches will be put down 200 yards S.E. of the enemy front line from N 14 d 3 5 to N 14 b 9 4 at Zero plus 5 minutes.

15. PRISONERS.
Prisoners captured will be brought to Battalion H.Q. by the men capturing them. Two men will return as escort to each prisoner captured.
Souvenirs must on no account be taken from prisoners.

16. MEDICAL.
4 Stretcher Bearers (to be supplied by Coys concerned) will be in readiness in NO MAN'S LAND in rear of each platoon and in rear of our wire by half an hour before Zero hour.
4 Coy Stretcher Bearers (to be supplied by Coys concerned) will also be in trench in rear of platoons by Zero hour.
Relay Stretcher posts will be established under orders of the Medical Officer at Front Line Coy H.Q. ("A" Coy 12th East Surreys). Coy stretcher bearers will many evacuate back to Relay Stretcher posts.

17. INSTRUCTIONS/

(3)

INSTRUCTION FOR FRONT LINE GARRISON.
17. The front line will be held as light as possible during the period the raid is taking place.

18. REPORT CENTRE.
An advanced report centre will be established in the Front Line at N 14 a 0 4.
Lieut P.J. WHALEY, M.C. will be at advanced report centre.
Platoon Commanders and Platoon Sergts will report at Advanced report centre after returning from raid and before proceeding to Front Line Coy H.Q. ("A" Coy 12th East Surrey.)
The following code will used for reports which can be sent from Front Line Coy H.Q. or from Advanced Report Centre:-

BOM	-- --	Raid a success.
R.R.	-- --	Raiding party has returned to our Front Line Trench.
M.	-- --	Missing. (No. of missing to be sent before letter).
P.	-- --	Prisoners taken. (No. of Prisoners taken to be sent before letter).
W.	-- --	Wounded. (No. of our wounded to be sent before letter).

19. ACKNOWLEDGE.

[signature]

Captain & Adjutant,
"BRAHOM".

Issued at 4-50 p'm. 22nd July, 1918.

Copies to :-
Copy No. 1 Filed.
2 Commanding Officer.
3 122nd Infantry Brigade.
4 12th East Surrey Regiment.
5 War Diary.
6 2/Lieut C. KILEBONE.
7 2/Lieut F.W. LEE.
8 Lieut P.J. WHALEY, M.C.
9 Lieut P.N. BOWSTEAD, M.C.
10 O.C. "A" Coy.
11 O.C. "B" Coy.
12 O.C. "C" Coy.
13 O.C. "D" Coy.
14 Medical Officer.
15)
16)
17) For N.C.Os. of Raiding party.
18)

The Officer Commanding　　　G 377
15th Batt Hampshire Regt
Headquarters
122 Infantry Brigade

　　　Herewith War Diary for the
month of August 1918.

　　　　　　　　　　　Lieut Colonel
Commanding 15th Batt Hampshire Regt

5/9/18

Army Form C. 2118.

WAR DIARY
15th Hampshire Regt.
or
INTELLIGENCE SUMMARY.
(Erase heading not required.)

Instructions regarding War Diaries and Intelligence Summaries are contained in F. S. Regs., Part II. and the Staff Manual respectively. Title pages will be prepared in manuscript.

Place	Date	Hour	Summary of Events and Information	Remarks and references to Appendices
HELFAUT	Aug 1st		Battalion arrived in front line by 4 of Canadians. Mounted Rifles and moved to Reserve in REMY area.	
	2nd		Battalion move by bus to HELFAUT, near WISERNES; arrived at 2 p.m. H.Q., C, and D Coys at HELFAUT; A and B at BILQUES	
	3rd		Rest and clean up. Young people taken out. Church parade in Y.M.C.A.	
	4th		Training of Battalion for attack	
	5th		Ditto — Day and Night operations	
	6th		Battalion left HELFAUT by bus and entrained to REMY; after dark marched to WEST-OUTRE bus where Coys to A up their assembly positions. Attack was carried out as had been planned. Forming up bus was midnight operation. On night out enemy at 4 a.m. of objectives we found we were the line to the left of D Coy; mistakes was stronger than anticipated and thus saw two posts had to be made about of objective line. C and B Coys had heavy fighting but about 60% casualties. A Coy sustained much less opposition. About 30 prisoners and considerable amount of valuable documents captured, including two A.A. Guns.	

Army Form C. 2118.

WAR DIARY
or
INTELLIGENCE SUMMARY.
(Erase heading not required).

Instructions regarding War Diaries and Intelligence Summaries are contained in F. S. Regs., Part II. and the Staff Manual respectively. Title pages will be prepared in manuscript.

Place	Date	Hour	Summary of Events and Information	Remarks and references to Appendices
	August 11th		Line consolidated and handed over to 18th K.R.R.C.	
	" 12th		Battalion marched to billets in LAPPE area.	
	" 13th		Rest and clean up	
	" 14th		Coy " " " and specialist training.	
	" 15th		" " "	
	" 16th		Battalion relieved 12th E. Surreys in front line. S.O.S put up at commencement of relief. Hostile party driven off and relief completed	
	" 17th		Fairly quiet tour. No infantry action.	
	" 18th		"	
	" 19th		A. and D Coys in front line.	
	" 20th		"	
	" 21st		Post nr Wilhelm Lamp advanced without opposition.	
	" 22nd		Battalion relieved by 18 K.R.R.C.	
	" 23rd		Attack on 18th K.R.R.C. resulting in capture of three posts.	
	" 24th		B. Coy went up to SCHERENBURG LINE to support 18th K.R.R.C in minor operation to retake posts. Only slight infantry action	

WAR DIARY
or
INTELLIGENCE SUMMARY.

Army Form C. 2118.

Place	Date	Hour	Summary of Events and Information	Remarks and references to Appendices
			Honours and Awards:—	
			Attaining:—	
			Sgt. Evans M.M. 10th August	
			Pte. McNevell " 10th "	
			L/C Barnes. C. Bar to M M 23rd "	
			Pte. Crowder E M.M. " "	
			" Puffett. E " " "	
			Sgt. Harvey A. " " "	
			Pte. Inman H " " "	
			" Hughes A.E " " "	
			" Yerby C " " "	
			" Walker G. " " "	
			L/c Barnes A. " " "	
			" McClemmick L " " "	
			Pte. Chalkcroft H " " "	
			L/c Lusk A " " "	
			Cpl. O'Brien J " " "	
			Pte. Crowder H " " "	
			" Curran S " " "	

Army Form C. 2118.

WAR DIARY
or
INTELLIGENCE SUMMARY.
(Erase heading not required.)

Instructions regarding War Diaries and Intelligence Summaries are contained in F. S. Regs., Part II. and the Staff Manual respectively. Title pages will be prepared in manuscript.

Place	Date	Hour	Summary of Events and Information	Remarks and references to Appendices
			Honours and Awards :- (Continued)	
			L/C Jacques J. M.M. 23rd August	
			" Hodges F. " "	
			Pte Bothart A.J. " "	
			" Rygg T. " "	
			" Hurst A " "	
			" Collins J. " "	
			(attached T.M.B.)	
			Cpl. Morgan J " "	
			(attached T.M.B.)	
			Capt. F.E. Leybourne Bar to M.C. 31st August	
			Lieut. J.L. Spencer " "	
			2nd Lieut C.J. Potter M.C. "	
			" A.A. Bradley M.M. " "	
			" H.W. Swain " "	
			Sgt Lomas E. D.C.M. "	
			a/Cpl. Kipping B " "	

Army Form C. 2118.

WAR DIARY
or
INTELLIGENCE SUMMARY.
(Erase heading not required.)

Instructions regarding War Diaries and Intelligence Summaries are contained in F. S. Regs., Part II. and the Staff Manual respectively. Title pages will be prepared in manuscript.

Place	Date	Hour	Summary of Events and Information	Remarks and references to Appendices
			Casualties for August 1918	
			Officers:-	
			Capt. J. H. Sumner Died of wounds 9.8.18	
			Lieut G. H. Wotherton Killed " " "	
			2nd Lieut A. W. White " " " "	
			Lieut C. J. Boreham Missing " " "
			" J. L. Spencer M.C., Wounded " " "	
			" G. M. Bowstead " " " "	
			2nd Lieut H. W. Lee " " " "	
			Lieut R. W. Cook " 16.8.18	
			2nd Lieut A. P. J. McSkie Sick. U.K. 14.8.18	
			Other Ranks:-	
			13 Killed 9.8.18	
			8 Died of wounds "	
			13 Missing "	
			101 Wounded "	
			(continued)	

WAR DIARY
or
INTELLIGENCE SUMMARY.

Army Form C. 2118.

Summary of Events and Information

Casualties for August (continued)

Other Ranks - (continued)

2 Killed 16.8.18
10 Wounded "
2 Killed 18.8.18
6 Wounded "
1 Killed 21.8.18
6 Wounded "
1 Killed 24.5.18
1 Wounded "
2 Wounded 25.8.18

Lieut-Colonel,
Commanding 15th (S.) Battn. Hampshire Regt.

Army Form C. 2118.

WAR DIARY
or
INTELLIGENCE SUMMARY.
(Erase heading not required.)

Instructions regarding War Diaries and Intelligence Summaries are contained in F. S. Regs., Part II. and the Staff Manual respectively. Title pages will be prepared in manuscript.

Place	Date	Hour	Summary of Events and Information	Remarks and references to Appendices
	August 25th		Battalion relieved by 23rd Australian Regt and went into WESTOUTRE LINE	
	"26th			
	"27th			
	"28th		Battalion relieved by 7th L.N.LANCS Regt. and marched to ABEELE Station and entrained at 2.0 a.m.	
	"29th		Arrived at LUMBRES 7.0 a.m. and marched to billets in SETQUES	
	"30th		Rest and clean up.	
	"31st		7 mile route march for the battalion	
			Appendix in Lies of casualties for month.	

Army Form C. 2118.

WAR DIARY
SEPTEMBER 1918
INTELLIGENCE SUMMARY.

(Erase heading not required.)

Instructions regarding War Diaries and Intelligence Summaries are contained in F. S. Regs., Part II. and the Staff Manual respectively. Title pages will be prepared in manuscript.

Lieut.-Colonel _____
Commanding 15th (S) Batn. Hampshire Regt.

Place	Date	Hour	Summary of Events and Information	Remarks and references to Appendices
WAMBRES	1/9/18		Battalion marched to SETQUES and entrained for ABEELE where it arrived at 4 P.M. and was billeted at 2 & L 30 (duration orders attached)	
ABEELE	2/9/18		Battalion left billets at 7.30 P.M. and relieved 106 American Infantry battalion in VIERSTRAAT – KEMMEL line	
VIERSTRAAT	3/9/18		During the afternoon two daylight patrols were sent out from Bn. One day before seen by the enemy after proceeding about 60 yds and held up by machine gun fire and forced to return having suffered a few casualties. An attempt to comply with Battn Operation order D.F.1 was unsuccessful owing to the fact that the post herein stated to be occupied by Americans were in possession of the enemy.	
"	4/9/18		Operations carried out on this date are described and attached with B.O.O. DF 3.	
"	5/9/18		No further activity. The battalion was relieved on the night of 5/6 by the 23rd Middlesex Regt and marched to billets in the LAPPE area the last men arriving about 5.30 A.M.	
LAPPE	6/9/18		Rest and cleaning up.	
"	7/9/18		Kit rifle inspection under company arrangements	
"	8/9/18		Church parade in YMCA hut REMY SIDING at 10 A.M.	
"	9/9/18		Specialist training & reorganization.	

Army Form C. 2118.

WAR DIARY
SEPTEMBER 1918
INTELLIGENCE SUMMARY.
(Erase heading not required.)

Place	Date	Hour	Summary of Events and Information	Remarks and references to Appendices
LAPPE	10/9/18		Specialist and Coy training	
"	11/9/18		" " "	
"	12/9/18		" " "	
"	13/9/18		" Baths and Gas test	
"	14/9/18		Church Parade at YMCA HUT REMY SIDING at 9.30. Entire French hut by M.O. Battalion left billets at 5.30 PM and entrained on light railway for the line relieving the 10 RWK in support. Relief complete by 11.45 PM	
In the line	15/9/18		Working salvage and burying trenches	
"	16/9/18		" " "	
"	17/9/18		" Battalion relieved 12 E Surrey Regt in the left front sector relief complete 1AM B+D Coys in front line A+C close support. Patrols sent out from B+D no enemy encountered	
"	18/9/18		Salvage + working parties. Patrols sent out from B+D salvage + working parties.	
"	19/9/18		enemy sighted	
"	20/9/18		Salvage + working parties. Patrols sent out from A+C. Patrol of C fired on by enemy patrol who then fled	

Lieut-Colonel
Commanding 15th (S) Battn. Hampshire Regt.

Army Form C. 2118.

WAR DIARY
SEPTEMBER 1918
INTELLIGENCE SUMMARY

(Erase heading not required.)

Place	Date	Hour	Summary of Events and Information	Remarks and references to Appendices
In the line	21/9/18		Battalion relieved by 5th K.O.S.B. relief complete at 11 PM entrained at HALLEBAST and proceeded to ABEELE by light railway where it was billeted	
ABEELE	22/9/18		Rest & cleaning up	
"	23/9/18		Route march by companies	
"	24/9/18		Company & specialist Training, address by Brig. Gen Weston DSO MC	
"	25/9/18		Battalion scheme.	
"	26/9/18		Brigade scheme.	
"	27/9/18		Company and specialist Training	
			Battalion marched to and occupied tilleto vacated by 23rd Middlesex Regiment. (Battalion Operation Order No 134 attached)	
LAPPE	28/9/18		Battalion marched to OUDERDOM - DOMINION CAMP area. Route Boeschepe Cross Roads, Reninghelst. Battalion continued march and started VERBRANDENMOLEN	28/I 28.a.
VERBRANDENMOLEN	29/9/18		Battalion formed Brigade Reserve. March continued at 9.0 a.m. Battalion reached 28/P.9.b. area.	
	30/9/18		March continued mid-day. Battalion reached 28/P.15 b & d areas	

JCBright?
Lieut.-Colonel
Commanding 15th (S) Battn. Hampshire Regt.

WAR DIARY
INTELLIGENCE SUMMARY

Army Form C. 2118.

September 1918.

Place	Date	Hour	Summary of Events and Information	Remarks and references to Appendices
	4th		Addendum. Ref Sheet 28.S.W.2. The preliminary arrangements & assembling were carried out in accordance with orders, but as these were given at very short notice Coy Commanders were handicapped & were unable to arrange all they wished to do. The attacking Coys were in position behind Chunise Trench at the appointed time 4.30 a.m. Artillery arrangements were not quite satisfactory as the barrage came down E. of the railway running through N.18.a & N.18.d to left a number of enemy M.G. posts on the W. of the railway safe to fire unmolested on our advancing troops. The Battn, in spite of being much disorganised by very heavy casualties by M.G. fire & enemy snipers, succeeded in reaching the line of the light railway, but were unable to hold it owing to the accuracy & strength of the enemy's M.G. fire & shortage of men. About dusk 2nd Lieut J.J. POTTER. M.C. collected & reorganised all the men that remained of the Battalion and established a	

Commanding 15th (S) Battn. Hampshire Regt.
Lieut-Colonel

WAR DIARY
INTELLIGENCE SUMMARY

September 1918.

Army Form C. 2118.

Place	Date	Hour	Summary of Events and Information	Remarks and references to Appendices
	4: (Cont)		Line from N.23.d.55.30 to N.17.d.40.40. & during the night got in touch with the 18th K.R.R.C. on his left, who had taken over from the 12th E. SURREYS. Casualties on this day were very heavy & included the C.O., and the Acting Adjutant. Officer Casualties 16. Other Ranks 307. Total Casualties 323.	

Lieut-Colonel
Commanding 18th Bn. Hampshire Regt.

Army Form C. 2118.

WAR DIARY
or
INTELLIGENCE SUMMARY.

September 1918.

(Erase heading not required.)

Instructions regarding War Diaries and Intelligence Summaries are contained in F. S. Regs., Part II. and the Staff Manual respectively. Title pages will be prepared in manuscript.

Place	Date	Hour	Summary of Events and Information	Remarks and references to Appendices
			Appendix II — List of Casualties September	
			Officers Killed	
			Capt. F.E. Leybourne M.C. 4 September 1918	
			Lieut. J.R. Toms "	
			2nd Lt. W. Feetham "	
			2nd Lt. H.C. Hull (Welsh Regt. attached) "	
			2nd Lt. J.H. Woolven (Wiltshire Regt. attached) "	
			2nd Lt. N.N. Mortimer "	
			2nd Lt. J. Prero "	
			Missing	
			Capt. C.C. Newman M.C.	
			Wounded	
			Lieut. M.W. Loveridge (1st Dragoon troops attached)	
			2nd Lt. A. Tubbs (Wiltshire Regt. attached)	
			2nd Lt. D.E. Carley	
			2nd Lt. L.A. Brown	
			Gassed	
			Lieut-Col. L. Murdoch D.S.O	
			2nd Lt. F.H.J. Dump M.C. M.M.	
			2nd Lt. A.A. Bradley	

O.C. Crick
Lieut.-Colonel
Commanding 15th (S) Battn. Hampshire Regt.

WAR DIARY
or
INTELLIGENCE SUMMARY.

September 1918

Army Form C. 2118.

Place	Date	Hour	Summary of Events and Information	Remarks and references to Appendices
			Appendix II List of Casualties (continued)	
			Officers (continued)	
			Wounded 2nd Lt. Heilbron 19-9-18	
			2nd Lt. F.G. Lawes 23-9-18	
			Other Ranks.	
			Killed 35	
			Died of wounds 4	
			Missing 8	
			Wounded 170	
			Gassed 3	
			Shell-shock 4	
			Injured (not classified) 4	
			Wounded 1 4-9-18	
			" 2 16-9-18	
			20-9-18	

Commanding 13th (S) Battn. Hampshire Regt.

Army Form C. 2118.

WAR DIARY
or
INTELLIGENCE SUMMARY.

September 1918.

(Erase heading not required.)

Place	Date	Hour	Summary of Events and Information	Remarks and references to Appendices
			Appendix "Honours and Awards"	
			119.13 C.S.M. PYM. R. awarded M.M. 15th September
			19407 L/Sgt. BEALE. E.R. " Bar to M.M. "
			19057 Sgt. BARTON. R.C. " M.M. "
			204773 Pte HENDRY. W.H. " " "
			204693 " ADAMS. B.A. " " "
			204807 " MASON. W.G. " " "
			28245 " BEATTIE. A. " " "
			33133 L/Corpl. ROGERS. W. " " "
			18537 Pte SIMMONDS. F. " " "
			45763 " TOWNSEND. H.C. " " "
			282254 Cpl. ROBSON. W. " " "
			7863 " DUVAL. C. " " "
			27029 Pte RIVERS. P.F. " " "
			205031 " JAMES. F. " " "

Commanding 13th (S) Battn. Hampshire Regt.
Lieut-Colonel

I.

The Secretary,
    Kent T.F. Assocn., MAIDSTONE.

    Herewith Part II Orders of the undermentioned
Units of the Royal West Kent Regiment, for your information
and necessary action.
    Please acknowledge hereon.

                                H Churchill Heap
HOUNSLOW.   for/Lt-Colonel,
25/9/1918.   i/c. No.2. Infantry Records.

Unit.	Numbers inclusive.	Station.
10 RWKents	T.52	B.E.F
11 RWKents	T.35	B.E.F

II.

To:-
    The Officer i/c.,
        No.2. Infantry Record Office,
        Staines Road, Hounslow.

    Above Part II Orders received.

                                G. Ashhurst /Secretary
                                Kent T.F. Association

From:　　　　　　　　　　　　　　　　　　　　　　　　　　L.R. 294

　　　Officer Commanding,
　　　　　15th. Batt. Hampshire Regt.
To:

　　　Headquarters,
　　　　　122nd. Infantry Brigade.
　　　　　　　　　　　————

　　　　　　　Herewith War Diary for the Month of

October, please.

5/11/17　　　　　　　　　　　　　　　　　Lieut. Colonel,
　　　　　　　　　　　Commanding 15th. Batt. Hampshire Regt.

15th Hampshire Regt.

WAR DIARY
INTELLIGENCE SUMMARY
(Erase heading not required)

Army Form C. 2118.

October 1918.

Commanding 15th (S) Battn. Hampshire Regt.
Lieut-Colonel

Place	Date	Hour	Summary of Events and Information	Remarks and references to Appendices
	1st		The Battalion were detailed as Reserve Battn to the Brigade & in accordance with orders, marched from Kronaers, 1 mile W. of TENBRIELAN to AMERICA. Here the Battn came under very heavy concentrated fire, at short range from the right flank, from the direction of NERVICQ. Some casualties were caused, including the C.O. & the Adjt, who were both wounded. At this time Capt. C.H.B. Good assumed command of the Battn. The Battn proceeded in Artillery formation to the vicinity of 28.Q.2. Central, where they halted. The enemy shelled intermittently till dawn.	
	2nd		Orders were received for the Battn to attack a line E. of the GHELUWE SWITCH, in conjunction with the 18th K.R.R.C. & the 20th Dur on the left. The attack commenced about 05.30 & proceeded well, inspite a creeping barrage, which was very effective. On the right flank of the Battn, one Coy penetrated as far as QUANDARY FARM, but from this very advanced position, it was forced to retire owing to there being no support on their flanks. The line which was finally established was QUARANTINE FARM —	28/5/19 2/5/19 3/5/19

WAR DIARY
INTELLIGENCE SUMMARY. October 1918.

Army Form C. 2118.

Commanding 15th (S) Battn. Hampshire Regt.
Lieut.-Colonel

Place	Date	Hour	Summary of Events and Information	Remarks and references to Appendices
	2nd (Cont)		FRENZY FARM. — QUARTER COTTAGES. Casualties were fairly heavy. 12 M.G's. & a number of prisoners were captured. At dusk the enemy heavily counter attacked the troops on our right flank & forced us to retire behind the railway to the line of the GHELUWE SWITCH.	
	3rd		About mid-night 2nd/3rd, the Battn were relieved by the 34th Div. & marched to billets at ZANDVOORDE, arriving about 0530. Later in the day orders were received for the Battn to concentrate at ROSSIGREL CAB, K.31. on the MENIN Rd. & from here they marched to bivouacs at U.23.d.	
	4th		Major Stoddard M.C. took over command of the Battn. The Battn remained in bivouacs.	
	5th		Orders were received to reconnoitre the line MOLENHOEK — ZUIDOOSTHOEK, as a reserve position, & one Coy were sent to occupy this line.	
	6th		Orders were received for the Battn to proceed to billets at HOOGRAFF CAB. This was carried out by a route march to YPRES & thence by motor buses.	

Army Form C. 2118.

WAR DIARY
or
INTELLIGENCE SUMMARY. October 1918.
(Erase heading not required.)

Place	Date	Hour	Summary of Events and Information	Remarks and references to Appendices
HOOGSTAFF	7th		The Battalion out at rest. The day was spent in cleaning arms & equipment. A kit inspection was also held.	
	8th		Battn at rest. Company training took place in the morning & in the afternoon, the Battn had baths & clean change of underclothes.	
	9th		Battn at rest. Coy & Specialist training	
	10th		Battn out on a Bde Scheme. (Battn Operation Order attached).	
	11th		Battn at rest. Coy & Specialist training.	
	12th		Batt at rest " "	

Lieut.-Colonel
Commanding 16th (S) Battn. Hampshire Regt.

WAR DIARY
or
INTELLIGENCE SUMMARY.

(Erase heading not required.) October 1918

Army Form C. 2118.

Place	Date	Hour	Summary of Events and Information	Remarks and references to Appendices
HOOGRAFF	13	9.30	The Battalion left billets and marched to REMY SIDINGS where they entrained for STIRLING (PSTIF) on detraining the Battalion had a hot meal at 4.30 p.m. then marched along YPRES-MENIN road to area J.2 & J.30 & 5.30 where H.Q. was established in a pillbox. Companies relieved 2/nd Middlesex in Support Line. At 5.30 a.m. the C.O. met Coy commrs and went to show them the position to be taken over, at conference was held at H.Q. at 3.00 p.m.	
	14		Companies moved off individually and assembly position was on. Companies moved off individually and took up assembly positions where the men had hot meal between 6 & 7. H.Q. established close to PAUN FARM in front of the enemy wire. Shel.29 B 9 8 to 29 B 2 D D O order of advance. The Battalion frontage was A.D.B. in second wave, A & C in front in two lines of section in file Battn in second wave, keeping Douve between the lines of A & C Coys. At 5.35 our barrage opened and the Battn went forward in a very thick, considerable opposition was encountered from Pillboxes at the commencement of the advance which were soon overcome by the dash and determination of the troops who took every advantage of the very heavy mist, which was the cause of some of the men of the other units running themselves up until we. In spite of mist	Spkill.s.b Lieut.Har.G X.O.

WAR DIARY
or
INTELLIGENCE SUMMARY

Army Form C. 2118.

October 1918

Place	Date	Hour	Summary of Events and Information	Remarks and references to Appendices
	16		difficulties the Battalion attained its 1st Objective according to programme, here the Tanks (2) passed through and went on to the 2nd Objective, then the advance was continued by the 13th Bgde pressing through. Posts were then established in depth on the 2nd Objective line Battalion HQ was established at K.26.d.2.1 On the morning the 112th Div. was ordered to relieve the 50 Div. the 152 Bgde being in support. Battalion marched to JASPER (ORDER K.21.C.7.4. and then via MOORSEELE and GULEGHEM to HERLE where the Bn. was billeted in houses in the vicinity G.23.a.9.8. The Battalion suffered 37 casualties by a direct hit of a shell on the GULEGHEM - HERLE road, 3 further casualties caused during the evening owing to shells falling near the billets Battalion remained in same place BHQ moved to the Chateau in HERLE.	
	17	0940	The casualties suffered by the Bn. in the battle on the morning of the 14th Oct. was 63 including 5 officers, rounded taken by the Bn. were 230 and 4 machine guns with 1 anti tank rifle.	

P. Kilpatrick Lt Col
O.C. 6th Bn [?]

WAR DIARY
or
INTELLIGENCE SUMMARY

Army Form C. 2118.

(Erase heading not required.) October 1918

Place	Date	Hour	Summary of Events and Information	Remarks and references to Appendices
	18		Resting at LISLE. Enemy shelling the vicinity with lachrymatory shells	
	19		Battalion moved on to BISSEGHEM and occupied the Rue Lys near the station where the Bn billeted in the area 20 near the chateau	
	20		Bn moved via COURTRAI to be billed in the vicinity of SWEVEGHEM. On arrival it was discovered that the enemy still occupied the allotted area, thereby the Bn was billeted on the road half way between COURTRAI and SWEVEGHEM.	
	21		B.O.D. of Bge. OO227 (attached) was carried out by the Battalion. On 10th Battalion arriving at knocke the bridges over the canal were found to be blown up; this delayed our unimpeded advance on the enemy who actived over the canal, but great gallantry dash and determination the Bn crossed the BASCULE CANAL AT KNOCKE under very heavy machine gun and artillery fire. A Coy taking the lead, the Bn was able to continue the advance for about 600 yds towards the SCHELDT, where they were held up for the night by enemy machine guns nests established on the ridge overlooking the SCHELDT area. Bn HQ was established at the Brick Kiln, SCHELDT area.	
	22		The Battalion continued the advance towards the objective but were held up by the enemy machine gun posts	S.P. Johnson Lt Col

Army Form C. 2118.

WAR DIARY
or
INTELLIGENCE SUMMARY.
(Erase heading not required.)

October 1918

Place	Date	Hour	Summary of Events and Information	Remarks and references to Appendices
	22		On the evening of the 22nd the 1 & 3 Bde went through and allowed us to withdraw to rest billets 600 yards west of Knocke and arrived on the morning of the 23rd.	
	23		Batt. in rest billets at O.21.	
	24		Batt. in rest billets at O.21. Off. 14.30 63rd Batt. moved to U.3 and in reserve to Division	U.3 were in Billets arrived at 17.00
	25		In reserve to Div. Off. 14.00 Batt. moved forward to U.18 & still in reserve. Billeted in farms.	
	26		Having by the 26th proceed to V.1 & 6 and concentrate there. C.O. and Officers made a reconnaissance of ground and reconnoitring patrols were sent out. After reconnaissance was made alignment was taken up from G.32 d 5.3 & 1.2 a 05. We had a take any front C Coy and D Coy in front were B + A Coys in second. C + B Coys on the Left D + A Coys on the right. The attack was supported by 4 Coy of 41st Batt. Machine Gunners, Trench Mortars and artillery. The Attack commenced at 16.00 without a barrage from artillery. On artillery fire was occasionally on targets which were holding up Machine Guns and Trench Mortars did valuable services and gave covering fire through the whole attack.	

WAR DIARY or INTELLIGENCE SUMMARY

Army Form C. 2118.

October 1918

Place	Date	Hour	Summary of Events and Information	Remarks and references to Appendices
	26		On our left, near the 12ᵗʰ E Surreys and on the right the Middlesex (23ʳᵈ) Commander was kept with Flanks during the attack. On the left C.Coy met with practically no resistance and went forward towards objective without casualties. After having advanced about 200 yds on the right "D" Coy were held up by machine gun fire from their right flank. A. Coy. who were in support to D Coy Nº made a platoon detachment with great skill and determination, cleared machine gun nest and came into the line with 03 & D.Coy. About this time the enemy put a barrage on our advanced troops which lasted for about 10-15 minutes. The heavy shells seemed to land behind. Regardless of the barrage "B" D & A Coy Commanders with great determination pushed their Companies forward so that the barrage was falling behind them. B. Coy who were in support to C.Coy met to heavy shelling and suffered slight casualties and were disorganised. B. O & A Coy's still pushed on successfully to the final objective clearing all before them and finally reaching their objective about 17.30 which was the line from G.34 & 3 Western main road to A.4.50.5. By this time B. Coy commanders then successfully reorganised and pushed forward to their position in support about 18.00pm behind objective. Coys having obtained their objective reorganised and got into touch with their flanks. By this time casualties had fallen. Posts were pushed 100 yds forward from our front line (2 per Coy) so as not to be surprised in case of a counter attack. The objective was a very commanding position along our whole front - steep Cliffs ...	

WAR DIARY
INTELLIGENCE SUMMARY.
(Erase heading not required)

Army Form C. 2118.

October 1918

Place	Date	Hour	Summary of Events and Information	Remarks and references to Appendices
	26		Saved the labour of digging in, only a few slits had to be dug in the ditch. The attack was a perfect success in every way, and the spirit of the troops was great throughout the day. Batt. Head Qrs. was at V.2.a.3.3. in a farm in the village of Uitkerdriesch. The enemy shelled the village heavily from 16:30 to 16:50, no casualties were caused. About 19:00 to 20:00 gas shelling occurred between the village of Trufflebeat and Kwestestreat. Chiefly lachrymatory shells from a S.E. direction. No casualties. The total number of casualties for the day was 20. 1 killed 19 wounded including one Officer.	
	27	21:30	the Batt. was relieved by the 18th Batt. H.L.I. and one Coy of the Royal Scots. The relief was very slow owing to the fight. The B.H.Q. at V.2.a.3.3. W.V.2.a.3.3. at 22:30 for N.24. We proceeded via Hooghe. REIBERG. KNOKKE & KAPPELLE MOLEN to N.24 where billets were prepared for us, we arrived at 05:30 and rest was the order for the remainder of the day.	
	28		Batt. at rest Billets in the vicinity of N.24. Company training.	
	29		Batt. at rest Billets in the vicinity of N.24. Company training.	
	30		" " " " " " " "	

P. R. Sebwig Lay
Lt. Col. 15th Hants

Army Form C. 2118.

WAR DIARY
or
INTELLIGENCE SUMMARY
(Erase heading not required.)

October 1917

Place	Date	Hour	Summary of Events and Information	Remarks and references to Appendices
	31st		The Battalion left their Rest Billets in the vicinity of N.3.4. and relieved the 18th H.L.I. & the 17th Royal Scots, of the 106th Infantry Brigade, 35th Division, in the Right Sub Sector of the Front Line. The 12th K.R.R.C. were on the Left. "A" Coy of the 15th Hants relieved the Left Front Coy "B" " " " " " Right " " "C" " " " " " Left Support " "D" " " " " " Right " " The Battalion marched to the Line via KAPPELLE — NILEANE — KNOKKE — HOSKE. Appendices attached.	

WAR DIARY
or
INTELLIGENCE SUMMARY.
(Erase heading not required.)

Army Form C. 2118.

October 1918

Place	Date	Hour	Summary of Events and Information	Remarks and references to Appendices
	19th		Appendix to War Diary for October 1918.	
			Decorations Awarded.	
			204571. Pte WEBBER. J. M.M. awarded Bar to M.M.	
	"		19074 Cpl. BISHOP. " " M.M.	
	"		28757. Pte NEATE. A. " " "	
	"		380196 " COLES. A. " " "	
	"		204403 Sgt. LONERGAN. J. " " "	
	"		28061. Cpl. FARR. G.H. " " "	
	"		250036 L/Cpl. TOWNSEND. E.J. " " "	
	"		27518. " BURRIDGE. H.S.P " " "	
	"		4176. Pte CHEEK. E. " " "	
	"		233342. L/Cpl NUNAN. A. " " "	
	"		10856. L/Cpl. POLINO. J. " " "	
	"		204984. Pte TAYLOR. S. " " "	
	"		204161. " HUNNYBELL. W. " " Bar to M.C.	
	26th		2/LT. G.J. POTTER. M.C. " " M.C.	
	"		LT. (1st/Capt) M.W. LOVERIDGE " " "	
	"		2/LT. G.H. SEAL. " " "	
	"		LT. C.V. HART. " " "	

Army Form C. 2118.

WAR DIARY
or
INTELLIGENCE SUMMARY
(Erase heading not required.)

October 1918.

Place	Date	Hour	Summary of Events and Information	Remarks and references to Appendices
	26th		LT. K. G. RAHAM. Awarded M.C.	
	"		26971. Sgt. BURCH. E. " D.C.M.	
	"		19057. " BARTON. R.G. " "	

S.F. Ackworth Maj
for O.C. 15 Hand

Army Form C. 2118.

WAR DIARY
or
INTELLIGENCE SUMMARY. October 1918.
(Erase heading not required.)

Instructions regarding War Diaries and Intelligence Summaries are contained in F. S. Regs., Part II. and the Staff Manual respectively. Title pages will be prepared in manuscript.

Place	Date	Hour	Summary of Events and Information	Remarks and references to Appendices
	2nd		CASUALTIES during October 1918.	
			Officers.	
			LT (A/CAPT) R.F. REYNOLDS. KILLED.	
			LT.COL. A.W. PUTTICK. M.C. WOUNDED.	
			CAPT. S.H. WIGMORE. M.C. "	
			LT (A/CAPT) F.J. WHALEY. M.C. "	
			1/LT. K. GRAHAM "	
			2/LT. G.J. POTTER. M.C. "	
			" I.E. WALKER. "	
			" P. D AYLWARD "	
			" V. HICK "	
	14th		LT. R.A. LEDWARD. M.C. "	
			2/LT. H.W. GREEN. M.C "	
			" K.F. CURTIS. "	
			" R.F.C. DARE. "	Since died of wounds.
			" H.G. SUMPTION. "	

P.F.Edwards Maj
L.O. "S" Hood

Army Form C. 2118.

WAR DIARY
or
INTELLIGENCE SUMMARY.
(Erase heading not required.)

October 1918

Place	Date	Hour	Summary of Events and Information	Remarks and references to Appendices
	22nd		2/Lt. W.V. COLYER. KILLED.	
			Lt. G. SABINE "	
			2/Lt. C.H. FERRIS. WOUNDED.	
			" G.H. SEAL. "	
			" B.W. DARKING. "	
	26th		" A.C. LANGDON. "	
			Other Ranks.	
			KILLED. MISSING. WOUNDED. DIED of WOUNDS.	
	2nd		19. 11. 120. 3.	
	14th		10. 2. 66.	
	16th		— 7. 4. 1.	
	21st		3. 1. 24. 1.	
	22nd		9. 2. 60. 1.	
	26th		2. 1. 16. 1.	
			43. 24. 290. 5.	

From Officer Commanding,
    15th. Battn. Hampshire Regt.   L.R. 893.
To Headquarters,
    122nd. Infantry Brigade.

            Herewith War Diary for the month
of November.

                                        [signature]
                                        Lieut. Colonel.
            Commanding 15th. Battn. Hampshire Regiment.

5/12/18.

WAR DIARY
or
INTELLIGENCE SUMMARY.
(Erase heading not required.)

Army Form C. 2118.

15th Hampshire Regt.
November, 1918.
Vol 31

Place	Date	Hour	Summary of Events and Information	Remarks and references to Appendices
	1		At midnight of the 31st/1st the Battalion relieved the 18th Batt. H.L.I. taking over the line from (Sheet 29.S.E) P.3.d.5.1 to V.9.C.2.9. A & C Company front was established A and B Companies in front line. C and D Companies in Support. A and C on the right B and D on left. On our left flank were the K.R.R.s and on our right a Batt. of the 21st Brigade.	
			During the early hours of the morning shelling was intermittent and at times considerable, but no casualties were caused.	
		11:00	C. Coy. who were in support were shelled causing some casualties.	
		16:30	Until this time all had been fairly quiet except for several rounds of machine gun fire. Six Hundred Gas Shells were dropped in the vicinity of D. Coy. causing 4 casualties.	
		16:50	Several enemy movements were reported from Observation Post which were forwarded to Brigade. Between the hours of 24:30 and 2:00 the Battalion were relieved by	

Army Form C. 2118.

WAR DIARY
or
INTELLIGENCE SUMMARY.
(Erase heading not required.)

November 1918

Place	Date	Hour	Summary of Events and Information	Remarks and references to Appendices
	1		1st Battalion of the London Scottish On completion of relief the Battalion marched to 29/W 18. 4.4. d. to rest Billets. Total number of casualties 8 other ranks. Officers Nil.	
	2		Battalion at Rest. At the Request of Company Commanders	
	3		Battalion at Rest. Company Training	
	4		Battalion moved to 29/J 31. to rest Billets.	
	5		Battalion moved to HARLEBEKE 29/H12 b. Heavy rain all day	
	6		Company Inspection and Specialist training	
	7		Company & Specialist Training. Baths in Klanen	
	8		Company & Specialist Training. Church Parade.	
	9		Moved to 29/T 29 d 9c. STERHOEK where we were in Reserve to Brigade who were in Reserve to Division	
	10		Continued march to NUKERKE 29/R 22 a 36	
	11		Battalion remained at Billets and found working parties for road repair from 29/R 19 a 2.6 to 0.24.C.0.4. Armistice took Effect at 11.00.	

Lieut.-Colonel
Commanding 1st Bn (R. Pen?) Hampshire Regt.

Army Form C. 2118.

WAR DIARY
or
INTELLIGENCE SUMMARY.
(Erase heading not required.)

Place	Date	Hour	Summary of Events and Information	Remarks and references to Appendices
NUKERKE	12		Working parties for repairing roads	
			A & B coys work from 09.00 to 12.30.	
			C & D " " 12.30 " 16.00.	
			A & C repair road from 29/R 14 d. 3.6 to 29/R 13 d. 7.4.	
			B & D " " " 29/R 13 d. 7.4. " 29/R 19 d. 2.6.	
	13		Working parties as yesterday.	
	14		Battⁿ move to area 80/O.26.	
			Battⁿ Parade 10.00. in order:- H.Q., Drums, C, D, A, & B. Coys.	
			Dress:- Fighting Order with soft caps. One blanket per man carried, rolled round the haversack.	
			All packs, surplus kit, etc carried in two motor lorries.	
			Battⁿ halted near BREVCQ from 12.50 - 14.00. Dinner	
			Reached billets at PARICKE 16.30.	

Lieut-Colonel
1/1st Hertfordshire Regt.

Army Form C. 2118.

WAR DIARY
or
INTELLIGENCE SUMMARY
(Erase heading not required.)

November 1918

Place	Date	Hour	Summary of Events and Information	Remarks and references to Appendices
PARICKE	15th		Coys. at O.C. disposal from 09.00 to 12.30.	
	16th		Coys at O.C. disposal. Special attention given to Saluting, Ceremonial Drill, Guard mounting, and a lecture given on March Discipline.	
	17th		Divine Service. C. of E. 11.30 in courtyard of PARICKE school. Nonconformist. 10.30 in day school, PARICKE. R.C. 10.00 in church, PARICKE.	
	18th		Batt'n moved from billets in PARICKE to OUERBOULAERE - LES DEUX ACREN area. Batt'n Parade 08.50. in following order :- H.Q., Drums, D, A, B, C. Dress :- Fighting Order, Steel helmets carried on haversacks, Soft caps worn.	

Lieut-Colonel

WAR DIARY or INTELLIGENCE SUMMARY.

(Erase heading not required.)

Army Form C. 2118.

November 1918

Instructions regarding War Diaries and Intelligence Summaries are contained in F. S. Regs., Part II. and the Staff Manual respectively. Title pages will be prepared in manuscript.

Place	Date	Hour	Summary of Events and Information	Remarks and references to Appendices
BIÉVÈNE	18th (contd)		Blankets and packs carried by lorries. Battn reached billets in BIÉVÈNE at 13.15.	
	19th		Coys. at O.C. disposal.	
	20th		Battn moved from billets to area EVERBECQ – GOEFFERDINGEN. Battn Parade 08.20. in following order :- H.Q, Drums, A,B,C,D. Coys. Dress :- Fighting Order as on 18th. Reached billets at 11.30.	
GOEFFER-DINGEN.	21st		Coys. at O.C. disposal. Battalion Concert 18.30	
	22nd		As on 21st – Training to include at least ½ hour's physical training.	
	23rd		Coy training as yesterday.	

Army Form C. 2118.

WAR DIARY
or
INTELLIGENCE SUMMARY.
(Erase heading not required.)

Instructions regarding War Diaries and Intelligence Summaries are contained in F. S. Regs., Part II. and the Staff Manual respectively. Title pages will be prepared in manuscript.

November 1918.

Place	Date	Hour	Summary of Events and Information	Remarks and references to Appendices
GEOFFER-DINGEN	24th		Divine Service.	
			C. of E. at 11.30. in Music Hall at GEOFFERDINGEN.	
			Nonconformists. 09.30. " " "	
			R. C's at 07.00. " Church "	
	25th		Presentation of Medal Ribbons by G.O.C. 41st Div: in field at EVERBECQ 30/U.9. a. 1.2. at 10.00.	
			"C" Coy represented the Batt: Other Coys: training as on 23rd	
			"Comps" Concert Party in Music Hall at 19.30.	
	26th		Coy training as on 23. Baths at the Brasserie. EVERBECQ	
			"Comps" Concert Party in Music Hall at 18.30.	
	27th		Coy training as on 26. Inter-Coy Rifle Competition commenced.	
			on 30yds range near Brick Stacks at 30/U.5.d.3.9.	
	28th		Coy training as on 27. Rifle competition continued	
			Inspection of Transport by O.C. 41st Div: Train.	

Army Form C. 2118.

WAR DIARY
or
INTELLIGENCE SUMMARY.

(Erase heading not required.)

November. 1918.

Instructions regarding War Diaries and Intelligence Summaries are contained in F. S. Regs., Part II. and the Staff Manual respectively. Title pages will be prepared in manuscript.

Place	Date	Hour	Summary of Events and Information	Remarks and references to Appendices
GEUFFER -LINGEN	29th		Coy. Training. To consist of 1hr. Ceremonial Parade and 3 hrs route march in drill order.	
	30th		Medical Inspection for all Coys during morning. Coy training to consist of Ceremonial Parade, Coy. Drill, Physical Training. Rifle Competition continued.	

Army Form C. 2118.

WAR DIARY
or
INTELLIGENCE SUMMARY. November 1918.
(Erase heading not required.)

Instructions regarding War Diaries and Intelligence Summaries are contained in F. S. Regs., Part II. and the Staff Manual respectively. Title pages will be prepared in manuscript.

Place	Date	Hour	Summary of Events and Information	Remarks and references to Appendices
			Appendix to War Diary for November 1918.	
			Decorations Awarded.	
	5.		45463 Pte E. TOWNSEND - M.M. awarded BAR to M.M.	
	12.		30481/3 Cpl. H. MATCHAM " " BAR. M.M.	
			6338 Pte F. HARDING " M.M.	
	15.		Lt. & J. POTTER . M.C. " BAR. M.C.	
	2.		Capt J.J. REYNOLDS. R.A.M.C. " " M.C.	
			T/Capt N.D. FAWKNER. A.S.C. " " M.C.	
	2nd		Lt. C. H. FERRIS ATT'D 15TH HANTS. " M.C.	
	2nd		HANTS CARBS. ATT'D 15 HANTS.	
			28493 Sgt-Major W. FOOKS " D.C.M.	

Army Form C. 2118.

WAR DIARY
or
INTELLIGENCE SUMMARY.
(Erase heading not required.)

Instructions regarding War Diaries and Intelligence Summaries are contained in F. S. Regs., Part II. and the Staff Manual respectively. Title pages will be prepared in manuscript.

Place	Date	Hour	Summary of Events and Information	Remarks and references to Appendices
			Casualties for November 1918.	
			Officers. NIL.	
			Other Ranks. KILLED WOUNDED.	
			NIL. 8.	
			TOTAL. 8.	

15th Hampshire Regt

WAR DIARY
or
INTELLIGENCE SUMMARY.
(Erase heading not required.)

Army Form C. 2118.

Vol 32

Place	Date	Hour	Summary of Events and Information	Remarks and references to Appendices
GOEFFERDINGHE	1.		Divine Services for all Denominations in the morning. Inter-Company football matches in the afternoon.	
	2.		Morning devoted to Company training on drill, guard mounting etc & musketry on miniature range. Afternoon to football & other sports.	
	3.		Route march which was to have been carried out was cancelled owing to weather, & companies were employed at indoor training & lectures by Platoon Commanders.	
	4.		Battalion football match against 12th E. Surrey Regt in the afternoon Lost 3-2. Divisional baths for all Companies	
	5.		Route march in marching order. Approx distance 8 miles.	
	6.		Company training consisting of Platoon & Company drill, physical training & guard mounting also eliminating practice on 30ft range.	
	7.		Morning devoted to cleaning & fitting equipment & marching order inspections by Company Commanders.	
			Battalion Strength:- 47. OFFICERS. 812. OTHER RANKS.	

December 1918.

WAR DIARY
or
INTELLIGENCE SUMMARY.
(Erase heading not required.)

Army Form C. 2118.

December 1918.

Place	Date	Hour	Summary of Events and Information	Remarks and references to Appendices
GOEFFERDINGHE	8		Divine Service for all Denominations	
	9		Route March in marching order. Approx distance 10 miles	
	10		Company training consisting of Platoon & Company drill, physical training & guard mounting	
	11		Company Training and Inspection for filling equipment and packing valises.	
CORQUAINE	12		Parade 0820. Bn. left GOEFFERDINGHE; back via GRAMMONT, VIANÉ, HERINNES to CORQUAINE. Very wet; no halt for dinner. Reached new billets 1430 hrs.	
SAINTES	13		Parade 1045. Bn. moved to SAINTES, arriving 1245 hrs.	
WAUTHIER-BRAINE	14		Parade 0930. Bn. moved to WAUTHIER-BRAINE : billeted in large factory. Weekly strength 47 Off. 798 ORs.	
	15		Rest.	
VIEUX-GENAPPE	16		Parade 0900. Bn. moved to VIEUX-GENAPPE via field of WATERLOO. Marched past the King of the Belgians who took the salute 3 kilo. before Bn. arrival at GENAPPE.	
VILLERS-LA-VILLE	17		Parade 0915. Bn. moved to VILLERS-LA-VILLE, arriving 1400 hrs.	
SAMBREFFE	18		Bn. moved to SAMBREFFE arriving 1400 hrs.	
ST. SERVAIS	19		Bn. moved to ST. SERVAIS, suburb of NAMUR, arriving 1400 hrs.	

Army Form C. 2118.

WAR DIARY
or
INTELLIGENCE SUMMARY.
(Erase heading not required.)

Instructions regarding War Diaries and Intelligence Summaries are contained in F. S. Regs., Part II. and the Staff Manual respectively. Title pages will be prepared in manuscript.

Place	Date	Hour	Summary of Events and Information	Remarks and references to Appendices
	Dec.			
WARET-L'ÉVÊQUE	20		Parade 0900. Marched to WARET-L'ÉVÊQUE.	
VIEUX-et-BORSET	21		Parade 0830. Marched to VIEUX-et-BORSET. "Final Destination for Winter Quarters."	Weekly
			Strength 46 Off. 776 O.R.	
	22		Reveille 0700. No parade.	
	23		No parade. Day spent in cleaning equipment and billets.	
	24		Morning given to company training. Education Officer opens classes. Lecture 1800 on "Scheme of Land Settlement" by E.O.	
	25		XMAS DAY. No parades. Festival duly held on actual Day.	
	26		Company training and E.O's. Classes. Voluntary classes excellently attended from the first.	
	27		"	
	28		"	Weekly Strength. 45 Off. 761 O.R.
	29		Company Training and E.O's. Classes. Bn. baths at WARRANT.	
	30		"	Bn. Cross-Country run. 1. LIEUT. C.V. HART. M.C. 2. PTE. HARTNELL, "B" Coy. 3¾ miles.
	31		"	Inspection of Bn. at work by Brigadier. Lecture 1800 on Demobilisation by Brigade Major.

WAR DIARY or INTELLIGENCE SUMMARY

Army Form C. 2118.

December 1918.

Place	Date	Hour	Summary of Events and Information	Remarks and references to Appendices
	2"		Appendix "I".	
			Honours & Awards.	
			Capt. C.R. BARBER awarded the M.C.	
			Lieut (A/Capt) H.R. REYNOLDS. A.S.C. " M.C.	
			31791. DEW. B. Pte awarded the M.M.	
			27018. HARRIS. Sergt (A/C.S.M.) " "	
			20800. SHIPP. Sergt " "	
			243245. BARKER. Pte " "	
			17886. BINSTEAD. L/Cpl. " "	
			204785. HAY. L/Cpl. " "	
			356089. MASON. Pte " "	
			874909. LIMMINGTON. " " "	
			204985. RIPPON. L/Cpl. " "	
			45581. BURDEN. Pte " "	

WAR DIARY
or
~~INTELLIGENCE SUMMARY~~
(Erase heading not required.)

Army Form C. 2118.

December 1918

Place	Date	Hour	Summary of Events and Information	Remarks and references to Appendices
	18		Appendix I.	
			CROIX DE GUERRE à L'ORDRE DIVISION.	
			11775 A/C.S.M. E. CROSS. D.C.M, M.M.	
			19414. Sergt W. LITTLE.	
			22983 " J. EVANS.	
			CROIX DE GUERRE à L'ORDRE BRIGADE.	
			350689. Pte J. MASON.	
			9471. Cpl. W. HUNT.	
			27018. Sergt E.C. HARRIS.	

LONDON DIVISION
(LATE 41ST DIVISION)
122ND INFY BDE

15TH BN HAMPSHIRE REGT
JAN - MAR 1919

15th Hampshire Regt.

WAR DIARY
or
~~INTELLIGENCE SUMMARY~~. JANUARY. 1919.

Army Form C. 2118.

Place	Date	Hour	Summary of Events and Information	Remarks and references to Appendices
VIEUX et BORSET	1919 Jan 1		Batln. observed New Year's Day as a holiday: no parades: Rugby football game in afternoon. "A" Coy (challengers) beaten by Rest 3 points to nil.	
"	2		Morning parades and Educational Classes resumed.	
"	3		Morning parades and Classes.	
"	4		Morning parades and Classes. Weekly Strength – 44 Officers, 736 Other Ranks.	
"	5		Church Parade in Canteen. Inspection of New Draft by C.O. Dance in Canteen.	
"	6		Morning parades and Classes.	
"	7		No parades or Classes. Day spent in cleaning and fitting for march.	
"	8		122nd. I.B. proceeded to GERMANY to relieve 3rd Canadian I.B. in centre sub-sector of left sector of X Corps front. Bn. marched to HUY, starting at 0715 hrs. entrained at HUY 1030. Transport started independently at 0615. Train left HUY 1220 hrs. Crossed frontier 2045 hrs.	
OVERATH	9		Bn. detrained at HOFNUNGSTAHL 0700 hrs. Marched to OVERATH 12 km. arriving about noon. D Coy at HEILIGENHAUS. A Coy at NEW HONRATH. B and C Coys in OVERATH.	
"	10		No parades. Day spent in cleaning equipment and billets.	

Commanding 15th (S) Battn. Hamp.... Regt
Lieut.-Colonel

Army Form C. 2118.

WAR DIARY
or
INTELLIGENCE SUMMARY.
(Erase heading not required.)

1919. JANUARY.

Instructions regarding War Diaries and Intelligence Summaries are contained in F. S. Regs., Part II. and the Staff Manual respectively. Title pages will be prepared in manuscript.

Place	Date 1919 Jan.	Hour	Summary of Events and Information	Remarks and references to Appendices
OVERATH	11		Weekly Strength Return :— 45 Officers, 817 Other Ranks. Posts established.	
"	12		B Coy find guards for posts	
"	13		C Coy find guards for posts. Educational Classes resumed.	
"	14		D Coy find guards for posts. Classes. New range started.	
"	15		B Coy find guards for posts. Range opened by C.O. who fired first shot. Classes.	
"	16		C Coy find guards for posts. Classes.	
"	17		D Coy find guards for posts. No Classes. Batln. has use of Divl. Baths in OVERATH and Clean Change of underclothing.	
"	18		B Coy find guards for posts. Classes. Baths continued. C Coy has use of Range.	Weekly Strength 46 Off. 835 O.R.
"	19		C Coy find guards for posts. Church Parade in Canteen.	
"	20		D Coy find guards for posts. Classes. B Coy has use of Range. Mounted Paper chase for officers; about 5½ miles; 22 2/21/23 including Lieut-Col. Brown and three other officers of 12th East Surreys; start from HQ Mess 14.35 hrs. Capt. Stobart and Lt. Livingston hors. Six minutes margin allowed. Hares make finish 43½ mins. First hound home 47½ mins. Capt. Bell, Brigade Signalling Officer, closely attended by Capt. Mowat, Hampshire Regt., Brigade Transport Officer. Third - First of Battalion	

Commanding 15th (S) Batln. Hampshire Regt.
Lieut.-Colonel

WAR DIARY
or
INTELLIGENCE SUMMARY
(Erase heading not required.)

Army Form C. 2118.

1919.
JANUARY.

Place	Date	Hour	Summary of Events and Information	Remarks and references to Appendices
OVERATH	Jan. 20 (cont)		Capt Oxborrow. 4th (2nd of Bn.) Capt. Fowler. 5th (3rd of Bn.) Capt. H.R. Reynolds. Minden finished course. Two fell.	
"	21		B Coy find guard for posts. Classes. C Coy have use of Range.	
"	22		C Coy find guard for posts. Classes. German Classes started. B Coy have use of Range.	
"	23		D Coy find guard for posts. Classes.	
"	24		B Coy find guard for posts. Classes. A Coy have use of Range.	
"	25		C Coy find guard for posts. Classes. C Coy details on Range. Weekly Strength, 45 officers, 831 other ranks.	
"	26		D Coy find guard for posts. Church Parade for Non-Conformists and R.C.	
"	27		B Coy find guard for posts. Classes. Bat'n. Concert Party open in Canteen.	
"	28		C Coy find guard for posts. Classes. Bat'n. have use of Dist. Baths. Clean clothing issued. Bat'n. Concert Party give repeat performance in Canteen.	
"	29		D Coy find guard for posts. Classes. Dist. inter-company Drill Competition. Winning Coy in the 122 "Brigade Group in this competition. "A" Coy. 15th Hants Regiment.	
"	30		B Coy find guard for posts. Classes. Company training started. C Coy have use of range.	

Weekly Strength

Lieut.-Colonel
Commanding 15th (S) Bat'n. Hampshire Regt.

Army Form C. 2118.

WAR DIARY
or
INTELLIGENCE SUMMARY.   JANUARY   1914.

(Erase heading not required.)

Instructions regarding War Diaries and Intelligence Summaries are contained in F. S. Regs., Part II. and the Staff Manual respectively. Title pages will be prepared in manuscript.

Place	Date	Hour	Summary of Events and Information	Remarks and references to Appendices
	31.		"C" Coy. found guards for posts. Classes. Coy training.	Weekly strength. 42. Off. 779. O.R.s
			HONOURS & AWARDS.	
	1.		BAR TO MILITARY MEDAL. 11775. C.S.M. CROSS. E. D.C.M. M.M.	
	17.		BELGIAN CROIX-DE-GUERRE. Capt. C. H. B. GOOD.	
	20.		BELGIAN CROIX-DE-GUERRE. 204673. C.Q.M.S. GREEN. G.F.	
			26872. Sergt. GROUT. A.G.	
			26938. L/Sergt. CHAMBERS. R.C.	
	23.		BAR TO M.C. Capt. H.D. FAWKNER. M.C.	
	24.		MERITORIOUS SERVICE MEDAL. 22963. Sergt. EVANS. J.	

Lieut.-Colonel
Commanding 15th (S) Battn. Hampshire r.

15th Hampshire Regt

Army Form C. 2118.

WAR DIARY
or
INTELLIGENCE SUMMARY
(Erase heading not required.)

Vol 34

1919 FEBRUARY

Place	Date	Hour	Summary of Events and Information	Remarks and references to Appendices
OVERATH	1919 Feb 1st		D.Coy finds Guards for boats. Educational classes. Weekly Strength 3 Officers 449 Other Ranks	
"	2nd		B.Coy finds Guards for boats. Church Parade C.of.E. and Nonconformists in the Canteen	
"	3rd		C.Coy find Guards for boats. Educational classes.	
"	4th		D.Coy find Guards for boats. Educational classes.	
"	5th		B.Coy find Guards for boats. Educational classes.	
"	6th		C.Coy find Guards for boats. Educational classes.	
"	7th		D.Coy find Guards for boats. Educational classes. A.Coy Lt.Col. Beard follows in Divisional Rifle — Company Drill Competition obtaining 550½ points out of a possible 635 points. Concert in Canteen given by 10th Queens R.W.S.	
"	8th		B.Coy find Guards for boats. Educational classes. Weekly Strength Officers 3B Other Ranks 452.	
"	9th		C.Coy find Guards for boats. Church parade to all denominations in Canteen. Winners of the Rifle — coy — Tug of War competition D Company. 5708 points out of possible 9100 points. Best shot 2856 2. L. Carter F. 40 bombs out of officers. 75 Ombs	
"	10th		D.Coy find Guards for boats. Educational classes. Inchelin commencement of Rifles — Platoon — competition. Draft 4 Officers 150 Other Ranks arriving from	

Lt. Hampshire Battalion

Lieut.-Colonel
Commanding 15th (S) Batt. Hampshire Regt.

Army Form C. 2118.

WAR DIARY
or
INTELLIGENCE SUMMARY.
(Erase heading not required.)

1919 FEBRUARY

Instructions regarding War Diaries and Intelligence Summaries are contained in F. S. Regs., Part II. and the Staff Manual respectively. Title pages will be prepared in manuscript.

Place	Date	Hour	Summary of Events and Information	Remarks and references to Appendices
OVERATH	1919 Feb 11		B. Coy. Find Guards for book. Educational classes. Baths & clean clothes for Battalion. Musketry Competition continued.	
"	" 12th		C. Coy. Find Guards for book. Educational classes. Musketry Lecture illustrated by slides given by Chevalier Tullio Sambucetti. Subject "Italy her relations with Great Britain". Vacancy allotted to Battalion Officer + other Ranks 60. Lecture was given at AUGUSTA SAAL, VOLBERG.	
"	" 13th		D. Coy. Find Guards for book. Educational classes. Musketry	
"	" 14th		B. Coy. Find Guards for book. Educational classes. Musketry.	
"	" 15th		C. Coy. Find Guards for book. Educational classes. Musketry Weekly Sergt. Officers 4 + other Ranks 806.	
"	" 16th		D. Coy. Find Guards for book. Church Parades. C. of E. and Nonconformists in Canteen. Roman Catholics in Church. OVERATH.	
"	" 17th		B. Coy. Find Guards for book. Educational classes. Musketry	
"	" 18th		C. Coy. Find Guards for book. Educational classes. Musketry Lecture by Commanding Officer. Subject Demobilization	

W. J. Partridge
Lieut-Colonel
Commanding 15th (S) Battn. Hampshire Regt.

WAR DIARY
or
INTELLIGENCE SUMMARY

Army Form C. 2118.

1909 FEBRUARY

Place	Date	Hour	Summary of Events and Information	Remarks and references to Appendices
OVERATH	1919 Feb 19		D Coy find guard for post. Educational class. Two tables. Double sentries mounted on all posts found by 1 Battalion. Officer in charge of each post until 1700. The Battalion also mounts guards over the river AGGER in their area.	
"	" 20		Officers examined all places of persons passing their posts.	
"	" 21		B Coy find guard for post. Educational class. Concert & Canteen given by Battalion assisted by Members of K.R.R. Concert party.	
"	" 22		C Coy find guard for post. Educational class. Two tables.	
"	" 22nd		D Coy Guard for post. Educational class. Weekly District Officers Hd. Qtrs Rumbo 423.	
"	" 23		B Coy find guard for post. Divine Service. C.of E. at Canteen. Tournaments at D Coy Concert Range of the K.R.R. "The Greenjackets" gave farewell concert in Canteen.	
"	" 24		Headquarters Guard found by A Coy. The Battalion relieved the Kings Royal Rifle Corps in the Outpost Line. A Coy at MARIALINDEN. C Coy at GRUTZENBACH. B Coy at FEDERATH. D Coy at MARIALINDEN. H Qrs at MARIALINDEN.	
MARIALINDEN	Feb 25		Headquarter Guard found by D Coy.	

Commanding 15th (S) Battn. Hampshire R.
Lieut.-Colonel

Army Form C. 2118.

WAR DIARY
or
INTELLIGENCE SUMMARY.
(Erase heading not required.)

1919 FEBRUARY

Place	Date	Hour	Summary of Events and Information	Remarks and references to Appendices
MARIALINDEN	1919 Feb 26		A Coy find Headquarters Guard. Conference by Educational Officer & Instructors was held at Educational Office, MARIALINDEN, to consider re-organisation of Battalion Educational system to meet present conditions. Use of the phrase "In-the-Field" discontinued in all Official documents, the actual name of the Place would be used.	
"	" 27th		D Coy finds Headquarters Guard. Educational arrangements made for early resumption of the Classes. Result of Inter-Battalion Rugby Match 15 Battalion Hampshire beats 18 Battalion King's Royal Rifle Corps. nil.	
"	" 28th		H Coy find Headquarters Guard.	

Capt. Acting O.C.
15th (S) Battn. Hampshire Regt.

WAR DIARY
or
INTELLIGENCE SUMMARY.
(Erase heading not required.)

Army Form C. 2118.

Place	Date	Hour	Summary of Events and Information	Remarks and references to Appendices
MARIALINDEN	1/3/19		HdQr. Guard found by 'D' Coy.	
"	2/3/19		HdQr Guard found by 'A' Coy. C of E service for A & D Coys & HQ at 11/15 hrs.	
"	3/3/19		Batt HQ Guard found by 'D' & 'F' Coys. Football match 15th Hampshire Regt 3 1/7 Middlesex Regt nil.	
"	4/3/19		Batt HQ Guard found by 'D' Coy.	
"	5/3/19		Batt HQ Guard found by 'A' Coy. Lewis Gun training carried out by 'B' & 'C' Coys.	
"	6/3/19		Batt HQ Guard found by 'D' Coy. Shorthand Classes resumed. Football match 12th E Surrey Regt 2 v 15th Hampshire Regt 1.	
"	7/3/19		Batt HQ Guard found by 'A' Coy. Shorthand & General Classes & Strength 'A' & 'D' Coys training. Football match 'A' Coy 3 v 'D' Coy 1. 599 Other Ranks	42 Officers
"	8/3/19		Batt HQ Guard found by 'D' Coy. Educational Classes. 'A' + 'D' Coys training	
"	9/3/19		Batt HQ Guard found by 'A' Coy. C of E service for A + D Coys. Football match 'A' Coy 3 v 'C' Coy 1/7 Middx Regt 1.	
"	10/3/19		Batt HQ Guard found by 'D' Coy. Educational Classes. A + D Coys training	

Army Form C. 2118.

WAR DIARY
or
INTELLIGENCE SUMMARY.
(Erase heading not required.)

Instructions regarding War Diaries and Intelligence Summaries are contained in F.S. Regs., Part II. and the Staff Manual respectively. Title pages will be prepared in manuscript.

Place	Date	Hour	Summary of Events and Information	Remarks and references to Appendices
MARIALINDEN	11/3/19		Batt HQ Guard by 'A' Coy. Educational Classes. A + D Coys training	
"	12/3/19		Draft from 5th Dorsets R & P. Batt HQ Guard by 'D' Coy. Educational Classes. A + D Coys training	
"	13/3/19		Batt HQ Guard by A. Coy. Educational Classes A + D Coys training	
"	14/3/19		Batt HQ Guard by D Coy. Educational Classes. A + D Coys training. Lecture by Mr Bee Mason on 'The craft of the Bee Hunter'.	
"			Strength 48 Officers 405 Other Ranks	
"	15/3/19		Batt HQ Guard by 'A' Coy. Educational Classes & A + D Coys training	
"	16/3/19		Batt HQ Guard by 'D' Coy. C of E service for A + D Coys & HQrs. also non-conformist service.	
"	17/3/19		Batt HQ Guard by A Coy. Educational Classes. Company Commanders Conference	
"	18/3/19		Batt HQ Guard by 'D' Coy. Educational Classes. 'A' + 'D' Coys. Provided working parties.	
"	19/3/19		Batt HQ Guard by 'A' Coy. Educational Classes. Working parties by A + D Coy.	
"	20/3/19		Batt HQ Guard by A Coy. Educational Classes. Working parties A + D Coys. Rugby match 15 Hampshire Regt 3 Lt amateur RH. H. A. C.	

Army Form C. 2118.

WAR DIARY
or
INTELLIGENCE SUMMARY.
(Erase heading not required.)

Place	Date	Hour	Summary of Events and Information	Remarks and references to Appendices
MARIALINDEN	20/3/19		Batt HQ Guard by 'A' Coy. Educational Classes. Working Parties by 'A' + 'D' Coys. Strength 46 Officers 649 Other Ranks.	
"	22/3/19		Batt HQ Guard by 'D' Coy. The Batt relieved by Oth Batt. East Surrey Regt. as follows.	
			'A' Coy. of E.S.R. relieved 'D' 15 Hampshire Regt at MARIALINDEN + BOHE	
			'B' " " " 'C' " " at FEDERATH	
			'C' " " " 'B' " " at GRUTZENBACH	
			'D' " " " 'A' " " at MARIALINDEN	
			HQrs " " HQrs " " at MARIALINDEN	
			Batts proceeded by march to HOFFNUNGSTAL + ROSRATH + VOLBERG.	
HOFFNUNGSTAL	23/3/19		Batt HQ Guard by 'A' Coy. C of E service for Batt. in VOLBERG Church. R.C. service in Bercalion Room. VOLBERG.	
"	24/3/19		Batt HQ Guard by 'B' Coy. Batt moved from LONDON Division to SOUTHERN Division. Farewell Message from Div Commander Entrained at HOFFNUNGSTAL. Departed 1556 hrs. Relieved by 17th Batt. Royal Fusiliers.	

Army Form C. 2118.

WAR DIARY
or
INTELLIGENCE SUMMARY.
(Erase heading not required.)

Place	Date	Hour	Summary of Events and Information	Remarks and references to Appendices
OPLADEN	24/3/19		Batt detrained at OPLADEN & proceeded by usual route to LEICHLINGEN	
LEICHLINGEN	25/3/19		Batt HQ Guard by 'C' Coy.	
LEICHLINGEN	26/3/19		Batt HQ Guard by 'D' Coy. Batt havre moved by march route to WERMELSKIRCHEN.	
WERMELSKIRCHEN	27/3/19		Batt HQ Guard by 'A' Coy. BATHS.	
"	28/3/19		Batt HQ Guard by 'A' Coy. Strength 46 Officers 670 Other Ranks.	
"	29/3/19		Duty Coy. 'C' Coy. All day devoted to cleaning up. 10 Officers 121 Other ranks reported to 2th Batt Hampshire Reg!. Drafts from 1st Dorset Reg! + Somerset Reg!.	
"	30/3/19		Duty Coy 'A' Coy. C of E service for Batt in WERMELSKIRCHEN Church. Lecture by Colonel Lawlw R.A. and Capt Weeks R.A.M.C.	
"	31/3/19		Duty Coy B Coy. A, B + C Coys parade full marching order. 1st copy of "Cologne Post" paper published and received south of Rhine. Officers + other ranks continue to make use of Bath.	

aupside